Investment for production

TO THAT MIXTURE OF HUMANITY:

MY FAMILY

Investment for production

Managing the plant investment process

Paul Lowe
Brunel University

A HALSTED PRESS BOOK

JOHN WILEY & SONS
New York – Toronto

Also by Paul Lowe

The Essence of Production David & Charles and Pan Books

*English language edition, except USA and Canada
published by*
Associated Business Press,
An imprint of Associated Business Programmes Limited,
Ludgate House, 107-111 Fleet Street, London EC4A 2AB

Published in USA and Canada by
Halsted Press, a Division of John Wiley & Sons Inc., New York

First published 1979

Library of Congress Cataloging in Publication Data

Lowe, Paul Henry.
   Investment for production.

   "A Halsted Press book."
   Includes bibliographical references.
   1. Capital investments. I. Title.
HG4028.C4L67   658.1'527   79-143
ISBN 0-470-26646-5

Typeset in Great Britain by
Photographics, Honiton, Devon
Printed in Great Britain by
Redwood Burn Ltd., Trowbridge and Esher

Contents

Preface

This book is concerned with industrial plant investments. Its purpose is to develop some aspects which are often overlooked and to put these into context. It intends to fill some of the gaps, known to many concerned with the plant investment process, particularly the engineers and the technologists who do much of the staff work which precedes or follows the investment decision. Their work is not well documented, yet it impinges directly on the well-being of most manufacturing companies.

There are reasons for such gaps in our knowledge. Perhaps the most important is that industrial companies do not seek the limelight of external scrutiny. There are enough problems already. Plant investments are, or should be, part of a company's strategy. This is a sensitive area and corporations, like people, do not rush to shed their 'seventh veil'.

Nevertheless, some glimpses can be had and here I have been lucky. The good fortune has been the chance to practise such work first professionally with a large company and subsequently to become an observer of the practice of others. For the latter I am indebted to various industrial companies which permitted me to get involved with a number of projects as if I were a member of staff, so that I could see their plant investment activities from within. Help with this study came from every level of management and the way in which it came was often instructive.

This book is a response to an opportunity. Its yield, I hope, is a systematic description of some aspects of the plant investment process which so far have been neglected. The account is in the first place intended for the operational managers and technologists who are involved with the various stages of the plant investment process. The approach, some of the concepts and techniques may help them with new insights into their roles. In some cases new material is blended with more established knowledge. Check lists at the end of most chapters are designed to encourage enquiry and reflection on current practice.

For the wider readership the main point is the growing complexity and importance of the plant investment process as technologies continue to advance. Investment is much more than finance at the right rate of interest or subsidy. Profound economic and technical changes are in progress. The further spread of automation in manufacture could have widespread repercussions in the next two decades. Many plant projects have an element of automation which further reduces labour requirements. Their success or otherwise will give an idea of what is to come. As the labour content of production (both manual and administrative) is reduced, effectiveness of manufacture becomes ever more a function of equipment and process technology, systems and scale of operation. Plant investment is an instrument of this change. Yet the human dimension can never be ignored and this makes the subject relevant to those who wish to understand some of the industrial problems of our times.

Many have contributed to this book, some specifically, others perhaps unwittingly. I am particularly grateful here to members of the various seminars on 'Investment for Production' organised by the Brunel Institute of Organisation and Social Studies. Their views, questions and, at times, disagreements were always stimulating and often instructive. My special thanks also go to Olive and Pauline Rolph for the smooth production of the typescript. Last, but not least, I am grateful to my wife for her patience in the role of grass widow while this book was written.

Brunel University
July 1978
                                          Paul Lowe

1 Introduction

The subject setting

The nature of the industrial investment process can be seen from two levels. The first is from the practitioner's point of view. Managers and technologists in manufacturing industry are frequently concerned with it as part of their professional work. Here, the interest is in the overview of the process and the insight this can yield, while the relevant techniques give scope for operational improvements.

The second level of interest is that of public discussion and government policy. The aggregate of industrial investment decisions is of public interest. The development of new industries and the replacement of old equipment with technologically-advanced production plant reflect policy goals which transcend political systems and levels of economic development. Industrial investments are an important factor in national economic growth, an aspiration espoused by most governments. Although the book pays more attention to the first level, the second is also borne in mind. The risks of such an approach are worth taking, because what goes on in its manufacturing industries matters to an industrial society. Their fortunes are too closely linked for it to be otherwise.

The process of industrialisation or the modernisation of

existing industries can be an uneven business. Success has varied with country and with industry. Many reasons can be advanced for the differences which often reflect an amalgam of economic, social and political factors. No answer based on a single-factor category is likely to be complete. There is a lack of systematic, integrated knowledge about industrial investment processes. This is an area of partial views and judgement is in terms of known components. The economics of the firm have provided theories, and forms of capital expenditure appraisal have furnished the techniques. On the other hand, organisational behaviour studies are still in their infancy. Systematic empirical investigations across a range of firms or industries are few in numbers. There is an unexplored interface between technology and economics, concerned with the decisions made by engineers and scientists. (Management does not make all the decisions.)

In essence then, the picture is incomplete and one object of this book is to develop some aspects of industrial investments which have not yet had enough attention. What this involves can perhaps be best appreciated by looking at the various approaches to the study of industrial plant investments. These are shown in Figure 1.1.

It may help the reader to have a brief explanation of the various subject approaches. Of course, all of them have their purpose and use. Some, however, need considerable expertise and experience. The specialist comes into his own; but study in depth can be qualified by a lack of perspective.

Economic theory. At the micro level this concerns the Theory of the Firm. In its simplest form this theory asserts that the objective of the firm is to maximise profits in the face of given market prices and means of production. The Theory of Production is concerned with the use of the various factors, such as labour and equipment, required for production and the scale of output. In turn, the Theory of Investment relates to the capital stock, i.e. equipment, involved in the process of production. The importance of these theories is that they provide a basis for analysis.

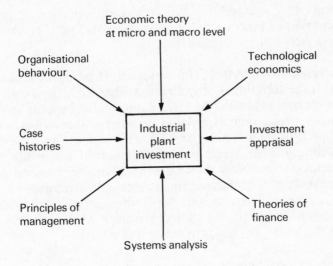

Figure 1.1 Some approaches to the study of plant investments

In macro economics Keynes[1] and his followers have emphasised the relationships between levels of investment, employment and interest rates. Ever since, investment has been regarded as an important factor in national economic and employment policies. Investment is also an ingredient in the theories of national economic growth. To put it crudely, investments are an important determinant of the wealth of a country — hence the limelight, the political debate and government measures which result from it.

Technological economics. These relate economic principles to the laws of science. A classical example of this is Kelvin's Law[2]. The scientific component of the law concerns the resistance losses of electric conductors. The economic aspects relate the operational costs of such losses to the original investment. An important application is the sizing of distribution systems. For instance, what is the most economic voltage for the distribution of electric power from a generating station? Technological economics are an important part of professional engineering work, yet they have had relatively little systematic treatment.

Investment appraisal. This approach is primarily concerned with the techniques of evaluation. Basically, the worth of a proposition is established by relating stated benefits to costs. Investment appraisal includes such techniques as Discounted Cashflow (DCF), return on investment and payback computations. Much published material has made these methods relatively well-known. However, second-order techniques which use these methods are not so well established. These include sensitivity analysis, risk analysis, simulation and the use of decision trees. Meaningful analysis at this level often needs to be computer based.

Theories of finance. These concentrate on the funding of investment propositions. Project cashflows are related to the cost and time scale of finance. This approach considers, typically, such aspects as equity/debt ratios, gearing, taxation and investment incentives.

Systems analysis. Industrial plant investments reflect a multistage activity — the plant investment process. Systems analysis examines its task constituents from the first plant feasibility study to the final project audit and relates these to the other functions of a manufacturing company. In many firms where plant investment is an intermittent activity the systems aspects have not been fully developed.

Principles of management. The means of manufacturing are, of course, fundamental to an industrial company. The application of accepted principles of management and proven practice to the plant investment activity can, therefore, be regarded as natural. Plant investment is an ingredient of business policy as well as operational management. Key management tasks such as planning, coordination and control feature prominently in the project systems which are the organisational vehicles for a company's plant investment programme.

Case histories. Because of the very complexity of major plant investment projects a number of research studies have been carried out *in situ*. This work has tended to be comparative to establish the character and structure of such projects in different industries. See, typically, Williams and Scott[3].

The organisational behaviour approach. This is interested in the individuals and groups of people directly and indirectly involved in the investment process. Just as a social anthropologist may study the customs and culture of far-off people, so he can work within a factory and observe what happens. The approach looks at investment projects in organisational, social and company political terms. It considers the effects of relationships, aspiration levels and value judgements. The experienced practitioner is intuitively aware of such aspects and their influence on both project survival and success.

The basic intent

(a)   Scope

The multiplicity of approaches to industrial investments outlined in Figure 1.1 indicate the many facets of the subject-matter. Some aspects are well covered; others are relatively neglected. The basic intent is to develop some of these neglected areas. They will not be dealt with in isolation but will be related to other parts of the spectrum of industrial investments. A perspective needs to be maintained.

The investment process will be viewed in systems terms. Particular attention will be given to the early stages of the process — the preparation of investment proposals. Investment appraisal has had considerable attention. The formulation of investment proposals, which is a prior activity, has not. If no proposals come there is nothing to be appraised. The latter activity is hostage to the former.

Plant investments will be seen in the context of technical change, much of which can only be realised when it is embodied in new equipment. This, in turn, is the result of research and development work. Plant investment is a partial function of this activity and this link is worth exploring.

It is an oversimplification to regard the investment decision as a yes/no choice once certain criteria have been specified. The decision process is essentially sequential with different people making decisions at different stages. These decision aspects will be explored. Also included will be the basic evaluation techniques and the more complex multi-outcome computations, such as risk analysis, sensitivity analysis and simulation. The basic decision of whether to invest in new plant has a number of cousins. These include plant replacement and plant leasing decisions. The alternatives confronting the decision maker here are somewhat different but, nevertheless, they are relevant.

The analysis is mainly concerned with the physical means of production, i.e. fixed assets in accounting terms. The installation of new equipment, especially for the expansion of production, may call for additional working capital, typically, for work-in-progress, stocks and debtors. This aspect is very important in its own right but it will be viewed here in relation to the central theme. Again, the financing of capital projects is most important but is not of first interest here. Readers who wish to take this aspect further are referred to such writers as Merrett and Sykes[4].

(b) Purpose

The emphasis of certain aspects within a range of subject-matter is governed by many considerations. Not least here is the development of material which is helpful to those concerned with the investment process in practice. At the operational level there is less time for the overview; the pressures of the moment usually come first. This book is, therefore, intended in the first instance for those managers and technologists in industry who are involved with some of the stages of the investment process - be this the preparation or implementation of plant projects. It hopes to give context and perspective to some of their work.

The second objective is to help all those concerned with the investment decision to improve their decision skills. This can be done by fostering a greater awareness of available alternatives, by introducing new techniques of evaluation and by making the formative project stages more explicit.

The general student of industrial investments and the lay reader may also find the subject approach of interest. Industrial investments - particularly by governments, where the taxpayer is an investor whether he like it or not - often reveal stark discrepancies between anticipation and realisation. Here too, it is hoped that the form of treatment will yield new insight.

Problems are not confined to frontiers. Those with industrial investments in the United Kingdom may seem serious to government and informed opinion. They are even more serious for some of the developing countries in the Third World. Aid to these countries, on capital account, has been substantial since 1945. See, for instance, the studies published in 1973 by the Overseas Development Institute[5]. Yet some of these investments have been mismatched. Insufficient account seems to have been taken of levels of education, craft and technician skills, local economic, social and cultural circumstances. The very level of technology seems at odds with its host setting. The new concept of 'intermediate technology' and the more systematic analysis of environmental factors which impinge on industrial developments reflect the measure of the problem. The imported investment is not always appropriate to the recipient country and the local student of industrial investments may find the description of the investment process of special interest.

(c) Method

The reader will note that the book has both descriptive and analytical chapters. Both are needed to do justice to a complex process. Techniques of evaluation require a mathematical approach. This is kept simple, but no apologies are made for using it. Reporting on a special enquiry into industrial innovation in Japan, conducted by the House of Commons Select Committee on Science and Technology, *The Times* of the 16 December 1976 uses the headline 'Inquiry into Japanese success is told that foremen are expected to know calculus'. The emphasis on numeracy has become necessary.

Wherever practicable, check lists will be provided to help managers and technologists to look at their own firms in a more structured manner. Furthermore, case examples will be developed to amplify particular points of principle.

The importance of industrial investments

Industrial investments are seen by many as a basic feature of modern industrial society. In some cases the commitment to such a view becomes an article of faith. However, should the yield of large scale investments — whether at the corporate or the national level — fall short of expectations, this faith can turn into disenchantment. Expectations, particularly expectations of growth — that compelling goal — will then be qualified.

Irrespective of outcome, industrial investments can no longer escape public discussion, be it on aspects of subsidy, taxation, jobs, pay, the environment or foreign competition. Underlying all this is the view that industrial investments are, and will remain, an important long-term factor in the economic well-being and growth of any society. Consider, for instance, the concept of economic growth put forward by Simon Kuznets[6], Nobel Prize-winner in Economics, 1971:

'A country's economic growth may be defined as a long-term rise in the capacity to supply increasingly diverse economic goods to its population, this growing capacity based on advancing technology and the institutional and ideological adjustments that it demands. All three components of the definition are important...'

The capacity to supply goods is obviously affected by the amount and nature of the available production plant. Advancing technology will mainly be embodied in it. Advance, therefore, often means the replacement of equipment. The institutional framework affects the attitudes to the required changes and becomes a determinant of their success. In turn, social values shape institutions. Given all this, investment is a subject for public concern. Yet, while government can provide by exhortation, subsidies and tax allowances a 'climate of encouragement' to invest, this by itself will not instal one piece of equipment. Technical staff and operational management still have to translate well-meant intent into successful plant investments.

International comparisons

Some indication of the contribution of industrial investments to the economic growth of a country can be obtained from national statistics. This is, of course, an important area of economic study but, as Denison[7] reminds us, caution is needed to appreciate some of the factors which affect such relationships. He considers the following to be the more important:

  (i) the quality of the equipment acquired in terms of their capacity for production;
 (ii) changes in the age distribution of the plant; this is affected by the retirement rate of existing equipment;
(iii) the gaps in the capital stock which are being filled. For instance, the removal of a bottleneck can result in an increase of output and income which is disproportion-

ate to the value of the capital investment;
(iv) the intensity of equipment use, typically, in hours per year;
(v) the allocation of capital to various industries with different capital intensities of operation.

Financial statistics furnished by the International Monetary Fund (IMF) allow appropriate comparisons to be made between the economies of the United States, Germany, Japan, France and the United Kingdom. Table 1.1 shows gross fixed capital formation as a percentage of the gross national product (GNP). This is then related to national indices of production. Ratios, not actual figures, are used to avoid the complications of fluctuating exchange rates. One cannot, however, entirely overlook the size of the different economies as these may have certain benefits of scale. Care is also needed with the use of the Gross Fixed Capital data as an indicator of industrial investment, as this includes housing, educational facilities and other non-industrial capital expenditures. Furthermore, no figures are available on capital consumption, i.e. the depreciation and scrapping of capital stock; the net fixed capital formation therefore remains unknown. Yet despite this, we are considering countries with broadly similar economic systems. It is also known, for instance, from United Kingdom statistics that the gross capital formation in plant and machinery is a significant component of the total fixed capital formation; typically between 30% and 40%. Whilst the percentage may vary for other countries, there would need to be a profound difference in the price structure and states of technology for this to be substantially altered. Empirical observations do not suggest this. It may thus be argued that the Gross Fixed Capital Formation can be used at least as a partial indicator of industrial investment.

Having made these various qualifications, what is there then in the data? Crudely speaking, the figures tell us the extent to which each country has 'ploughed back' its national product and to what degree its industrial output has in-

Table 1.1 Rates of capital formation and growth of industrial production, 1966-76

		1966	1968	1970	1972	1974	1976
Germany	Capital formation rate (%)	25.8	23.2	25.6	25.9	21.9	20.7
	Index of production	76.8	83.4	100.0	106.3	109.9	112.0
Japan	Capital formation rate (%)	31.0	33.5	35.0	34.5	34.2	29.9
	Index of production	55.0	75.6	100.0	110.1	123.3	124.7
France	Capital formation rate (%)	24.8	25.0	23.4	23.6	24.5	23.0
	Index of production	78.1	83.4	100.0	111.0	123.0	123.0
U.S.A.	Capital formation rate (%)	—	—	17.3	18.3	18.0	15.1
	Index of production	91.8	99.1	100.0	111.0	119.9	120.4
U.K.	Capital formation rate (%)	17.9	18.6	18.3	18.3	20.0	18.7
	Index of production	91.1	96.8	100.0	102.6	106.4	102.3

Notes 1. Data based on International Financial Statistics. International Monetary Fund February 1978 and May 1973

2. Capital formation rate is the gross fixed capital formation expressed as a percentage of gross national product.

3. Index of industrial production is based on 1970 = 100

creased. Obviously, there are other contributors to growth in output, apart from industrial investments. Nevertheless, the message is clear. The figures highlight the growth of the Japanese economy. National output more than doubled over the decade 1966-76, while the rate of capital formation remained well ahead of other industrial countries. Understandably, this astonishing performance has attracted enquiry into the sources of such growth, the impact of which is even more telling over a longer time scale. For instance, Denison and Chung[8] estimate that over the period 1953-71 the Japanese national income grew at an annual rate of 8.81%, which compounds to an overall growth of 457% for the period. Because of period differences, comparisons with other countries can only be indicative; nevertheless, they remain significant. For example, their estimate for the United States' growth rate (1948-69) amounts to 4% per annum, while that for the United Kingdom (1950-62) comes to 2.38% per annum.

Denison and Chung dissect the Japanese growth rate of 8.81% per annum and indicate the following main constituents:

Labour input	1.85%
Capital input	2.10%
Advances in knowledge, etc.	1.97%
Improved resource allocation	0.95%
Economies of scale	1.94%

The Japanese capital input effect is greater than that for any of the other ten industrial countries included in their analysis. The labour input and resources allocation effects reflect some structural aspects and changes in the Japanese economic system. Particularly telling in our context are the contributions from advances in knowledge and the economies of scale. They indicate the setting and the application of industrial investments. It can be seen that the overall amount of industrial investment is most important, but it is not the whole tale. Where and how much to invest, also what to leave alone, i.e. the strategy of investment planning, is also significant and its benefit can accrue both at corporate and at national level. The advance of knowledge component is an indicator of the extent and the speed with which innovations are incorporated in manufacturing operations. In Japan the gap between 'actual' and 'best' practice is small.

The Japanese success is instructive to the rest of the world. Some of its social and cultural components are not readily transferable to other societies. They would not be acceptable, for instance, in the United Kingdom. Yet much remains which could be adopted with profit.

In some cases plant investments are simple and straightforward. But where the scale is large and the changes big the plant investment process becomes complex. When its implications are underestimated, be this in a technical or an industrial relations context, the project outcome may be qualified. If results discourage and the experience is multiplied, national growth figures will reflect this.

There is need for a fuller view of the plant investment process — so much can depend on it. This book hopes to meet some of the need.

References

1. Keynes, J.M., *The General Theory of Employment, Interest and Money,* Macmillan, (London, 1936)
2. Thompson, W., (Lord Kelvin), *'On the Economy of Metal in Conductors of Electricity.'* Report of the British Association for the Advancement of Science. Section A. (September 1881)
3. Williams, B.R. and Scott, W.P., *Investment Proposals and Decisions,* Allen & Unwin, (London, 1965)
4. Merrett, A.J. and Sykes, A., *The Finance and Analysis of Capital Projects,* Longmans, (London, 1963)
5. Overseas Development Institute (editor Bruce Dinwiddy), *Aid Performance and Development Policies of Western Countries,* Praeger Publishers, (New York, 1973)

6. Kuznets, S. *'Population, Capital and Growth', Selected Essays,* (Nobel Memorial Lecture, 1971) Heinemann Educational Books (London, 1974)

7. Denison, E.F., *Why Growth Rates Differ,* Brookings Institution (Washington, D.C., 1967)

8. Denison, E.F., and Chung, W.K., *How Japan's Economy Grew So Fast,* Brookings Institution, (Washington, D.C., 1976)

2 The plant investment process

This chapter takes a first view at investment in production plant at the level of the company. To start with, the meaning of production plant will be more fully developed. The diverse activities and decision stages which form the plant investment process are then integrated within a systems approach. The planning and implementation of plant investment propositions goes on within the framework of company policies; the link, therefore, between the directing level and execution on 'capital account' is of special interest. Similarly, attention needs to be given to the interaction between those engaged on capital projects and those involved at various levels with day-to-day operations.

Where appropriate, discussions of principle will be amplified in this and following chapters by illustrations drawn from relevant industrial and research experience. The writer had the good fortune of access to plant investment work at a number of manufacturing companies. Reference will be made to work with four major companies. Two of these, companies A and B, are in the engineering industry, company C is in the glass industry, while company D is engaged in food production. The published accounts of these companies suggest that they belong to the more successful sector of their industries if such standing is measured in terms of size, profit and return on capital. All had large capital expenditure programmes. Although there were significant differences in procedures between the companies, each had given considerable thought to the management of its investment process and had evolved a standard practice.

The meaning of industrial investment

Anyone who has observed the pattern of expenditure of an industrial firm will note the variety of goods and services which it obtains in the normal course of business. Disregarding such day-to-day operational payments as for materials, of salaries and other routine disbursements related to the process of manufacture, one can discern a variety of expenditures associated with a longer-term intent. These constitute investments in some form. The following is a brief summary of the more important categories of such expenditure:

    (i) the purchase of production plant and the manufacture of tools;
    (ii) the acquisition of land and the purchase or erection of buildings such as factories, warehouses, offices;
    (iii) the purchase of all types of vehicles;
    (iv) the acquisition of 'administrative aids', such as computers;
    (v) planned increases in stock levels;
    (vi) research and development projects;
    (vii) the acquisition of patents and manufacturing licences;
    (viii) investments in or the acquisition of other firms;
    (ix) general portfolio investment.

All these categories have a common characteristic: they consist of expenditures from which future benefits or revenues are expected. The motivation for the expenditure is the criterion; future benefits may not always be realised. Except perhaps, for (v) and (vi) the firm usually requires capital funds for such expenditures, hence the term: capital expenditure.

In the United Kingdom, in accordance with Schedule 2 of the Companies Act 1967, companies are required to identify separately in their balance sheets fixed assets, current assets and those assets which are neither fixed nor current. In accounting terms it is the acquisition of these assets which can be regarded as investment. The term *capital expenditure,* as a sub-category of investment, will henceforth be confined to the acquisition, improvement or modification of fixed assets.

Investment for production

As to the investment expenditures already listed, this book confines itself to the capital expenditures which have some relevance to production. Production is taken here to include all those manufacturing tasks, including packaging, which make an article ready for sale within the normal practice of an industry. The transport or storage of finished products, as part of the distribution function, is excluded from this. The expenditures may be directly related to production, such as the purchase of machines, or indirectly in the form of building projects to house such equipment. Some categories are partially relevant; for instance, vehicles could comprise lorries for inter-factory transport and thus be directly concerned with production or they could be vans for retail distribution.

Administrative investments, say in computers and computer systems, tend to cut across functional boundaries. Admittedly, a computer specifically installed for the purpose of process control or production control is immediately relevant, but the majority of computers in industry tend to be applied first to accounting and commercial routines and to furnish general management information. Established originally in these activities, there is a tendency to broaden their role to the functional area of production. In many instances such widening of application was part of the original but not necessarily quantified purchase justification. The advent of the micro-processor is likely to bring computers much closer to production. Their relatively modest cost permits the development of decentralised computer systems containing a number of such units. This will be helped by the growing number of production staff trained in their operation.

Research and development expenditure, if capitalised, is relevant as far as it applies to production processes and leads to new or revised types of plant. This refers particularly to detailed machine design which can be expensive in draughting hours. Fundamental product investigations, although likely to have manufacturing repercussions, are not included. Again, investments in, or the acquisition of, other firms are only relevant if the objectives are related to production, such as the need to extend manufacturing capacity.

It is interesting to relate this approach to the national statistics relating to fixed capital expenditure of manufacturing industry. Table 2.1 indicates that about 76% of fixed capital expenditure is devoted to plant and machinery. The expenditure on new building work, at 18%, is relatively modest. Such expenditures are mainly a function of new factory building or major capacity expansion programmes. Often increased output, due to more up-to-date equipment, needs no more operating space than the previous process. The constant 1970 prices reveal the decline in the volume of investment which has taken place since that year.

The plant investment process

This consists of all the activities concerned with plant investment. The process starts with tentative ideas and finishes with their ultimate realisation in terms of effective, operating pro-

Table 2.1 Fixed capital expenditure of UK manufacturing industry at 1970 prices (£ million)

Year	Total	Plant and machinery	New building work	Vehicles
1968	1851	1406	336	109
1969	1978	1472	390	116
1970	2130	1624	391	115
1971	1991	1520	357	113
1972	1739	1310	306	123
1973	1753	1333	289	131
1974	2028	1529	359	140
1975	1745	1337	303	105
1976	1659	1298	240	121

Source: 'Trade and Industry' (Vol. 29 No. 9, 2 December 1977)

duction plant. The various process constituents are shown in a simplified form in Figure 2.1. They form part of the three main process stages: preparation, decision and implementation.

The illustration describes the cycle of a particular investment project. Where the scale and cost of a project is small (say, less than £25000) some of these stages are often further condensed. The various steps can still be discerned, albeit in an embryo form, and will not be overlooked by good project management. On the other hand, the bigger the project the more explicit, sub-divided and formalised are the various stages likely to be. The three main stages are, of course, sequential, with the output of one stage forming part of the input for the next stage and there may be substantial time gaps between the stages in practice. The process can be stopped at any stage but with increasing costs as it develops.

The plant investment process has a number of important characteristics which influence the effectiveness of its operation:

Discontinuity. The plant investment process stops with the successful operation of new equipment. By comparison, the main activities of a manufacturing business such as production and marketing are essentially on-going tasks. Organisation structures and working procedures express their relative permanence. In many firms, especially if they are small, investment in new production plant is a comparatively intermittent, temporary affair. Project procedures tend to reflect this. If they exist at all, they are often *ad hoc* in structure and intended to deal with a specific situation. The 'administrative tooling-up costs' are difficult to justify unless there is a regular stream of project opportunities. The higher frequency of projects where companies have substantial investment programmes encourages the development of standard practices. These tend to concentrate on the manner of project evaluation and submission.

The formation and maintenance of a project team can also be a problem. At its simplest level an operational manager or staff technologist may be given project responsibilities in addition to his regular duties. Such work may be spare-time by nature and correspond to the 'shopping basket' purchase of minor, standard equipment. In these cases no organisational dispositions are required; there is sufficient organisational slack (spare staff capacity) to accommodate such tasks. As we shall see in the next chapter, this usually covers only a small part of a firm's capital expenditure.

As soon as the project content requires full-time secondment what happens to the role previously filled by the new project engineer? Will he return to his permanent role when the assignment is completed and where, in that case, should his substitute in that role be placed? Intermittent project work will, therefore, cause periodic organisational adjustments. This can be compounded where the technical background of the project engineer is important; different plant projects could involve different specialists such as a metallurgist for a new plating plant, a paint technologist for a new printing line, etc.

An important benefit of scale is realised when the level of plant investments is sufficient to sustain a permanent project group. Typically, there could be a core team of project staff

Stage	Input	Process	Output
1 Preparation	Stimuli Terms of reference Standard data Staff resources	Proposition Development and Justification	Capital expenditure Proposal 'X'
2 Decision	Proposal 'X' Objectives Policies Financial accounts Forecasts	Authorisation Decision	Instructions to proceed with project
3 Implementation	Project brief Finance Organisational resources	Design Procurement Construction Commissioning Outcome Evaluation	Effective production plant

Figure 2.1 An overall systems concept of the plant investment process

which is reinforced as required by work load and mix. The
problem of discontinuity can be resolved to a large degree.
Nevertheless, here too, fluctuations in work load can still
cause severe difficulties and companies often go to great
lengths to keep project teams together.

Division of labour. Consider any project of substance, such
as the extension of a factory or the installation of new production processes. The project could involve such diverse
activities as design, plant specification, purchasing,
forecasting, estimating, costing, site work, plant
commissioning, etc. With these come a series of specialists
each making decisions in his area of competence. The
specialists may be part of the project team or, with lesser
schemes, retain membership of corresponding functional
departments, e.g. project costing by the factory management
accountant. Decisions which are made at detail specialist or

operational levels are encapsulated in investment proposals. Unless top managers keep in close touch with project groups their decision can be limited to a yes/no choice of one or a small number of 'homogenised investment proposals'. The division of labour between the preparation/implementation stages and the overall project authorisation decision can have some important consequences. Quite often we get different groups of people ill-aligned with each other. They make different assumptions and work within different information systems. This can lead to the fear by top management that engineers tend to 'gold-plate' their equipment proposals. Engineers, in turn, often feel that the board does not do justice to the needs of effective manufacturing operations. We have partial truths here. The important thing for management, however, is to realise the implications of this natural and necessary work division and to guide the investment process accordingly.

The need for integration. Consider further the case of a factory expansion and look at its possible operational implications. Take the ostensibly simple question: How big an increase in capacity shall we have? Immediate derivatives of this question, typically, are:

  (i) capital costs,
  (ii) economy of scale on capital and revenue accounts,
  (iii) expected sales,
  (iv) expected contribution,
  (v) plant utilisation levels,
  (vi) working capital requirements,
  (vii) manpower and training requirements, etc.

How are these separate aspects integrated? The project manager — the individual responsible for the task of preparation or implementation, whatever his title in an organisation — will have to harmonise and integrate the different specialist constrictions. That task is at the detailed project level. But there needs to be a much deeper integration — at the level of corporate intent. For instance, a given degree of expansion can be interpreted in different or even conflicting ways by various functional managers. The sales manager sees the expansion as an opportunity to challenge an entrenched competitor. The works manager sees the same project as a justification for a new maintenance building. The bigger the project the greater is the need for the integration of intent in terms of corporate plans. Even with smaller projects, such as the replacement of individual machines, the cumulative second-order effects require an overview, an integration.

Plant investment: the agent of change. As we shall see in the next chapter, plant investment is a major vehicle of change. It embodies innovation. The changes it may bring can, of course, be far more subtle and complex than the visual impact of new equipment. New plant, even if similar to what it replaces, represents a discontinuity in an operational sense. It impinges on aspirations and fears, gives bargaining opportunities, qualifies existing systems, causes new headaches. These effects are, however, not always pathological. Change will take place eventually in any case, with or without investment except that in the latter case it might be much more uncomfortable. The recognition and utilisation of this association with change will make the overall management of the plant investment process correspondingly more effective.

The project experience feedback loop. Figure 2.1 shows the output of the project implementation stage as 'effective production plant'. This is a physical condition where plant performance is related to set criteria. The means of verification is the project audit which will be discussed in Chapter 12. The project which has turned out well in all respects is not likely to be the subject of detailed scrutiny. This reflects the principle of management by exception. However, there are plenty of projects which do not reach this level, and their imperfections provide the learning opportunity. The experience can be utilised for future projects; Figure 2.2 illustrates such a notion of experience transfer. The experience may reflect shortcomings in project administration or control, contractual, technical or plant operational problems, in fact every aspect which affects project success. The feedback can be formal in 'inquest' and instruction terms. It may be informal yet still be quite definite, such as a senior manager's resolution never to go to a certain contractor again. The effectiveness of this learning process depends on the formulation of experience (project audit), the management system for capital project work and the ease of information transfer between working groups. Where substantial investment programmes result in a large number of projects, say over 100 a year, there is usually a continuity of comparative projects which facilitates experience transfer to subsequent work. The yield is less where significant projects (over £10000) are only occasional; memories fade and staff change. Again, where a company assigns much of its project work to consultants or 'main contractors' the internal experience yield will also be reduced.

Plant investment and the corporate intent

The relationship between plant investment and corporate intent can be most important. This warrants an examination of how the plant investment process fits into the total company system. From this point of view projects can be divided into three categories:

(i) The major strategic project to which the fortunes or even the survival of the company may be hostage.
(ii) The small, relatively routine project covered by regular budget provision, such as the use of depreciation funds for plant replacement. The project itself may not be of great significance at the corporate level. However, the category or group to which it belongs is important as an expression of company intent.
(iii) The 'conglomerate project' which fits neither of these

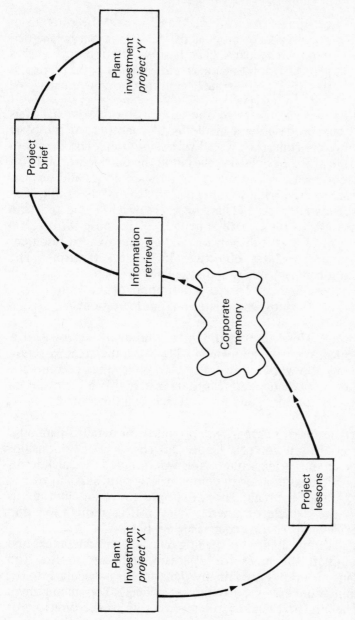

Figure 2.2   The project experience loop

categories. As a 'special case' — and there are a surprisingly large number of these — it can be the destroyer of systems. (The best way to approach such a project from a management/systems point of view is to divide it into strategic and routine constituents.)

What then is meant by the term: corporate intent? It is used here to describe a hierarchy of concepts. At the basic level we are concerned with *business purpose*. This describes the role of the business in relation to the outside world. In an economic sense it is expressed in terms of goods and services offered to meet a known or expected demand. Next, *business objectives* are a set of aims or goals which give a practical expression to the overall statement of purpose. *Strategy* is concerned with the disposition and arrangement of resources to achieve business objectives in a market setting. The definition of objectives and strategies provides the basis for policy development. Urwick's definition[1] of the term 'policy' is perhaps the most comprehensive interpretation:

Policy. This expresses the broad outline of the course it is hoped to pursue and which will govern the detailed action of all who work to the policy. The policy then becomes the governing theory and reappears in a modified form at each level of authority and for each technical function.

Thus, terms of reference are provided for detailed planning, execution and control. Figure 2.3 shows the relationships between the various concepts. It will be noted that such terms as profit maximisation or company long-term survival are not part of the hierarchy. They are hoped-for results, but not as such the vehicle of intent. They reflect motivation and provide both criteria and measuring sticks.

The responsibility for spelling out the corporate intent and making it the basis for operation belongs to the 'top management' of the company. This applies particularly to the formulation and authorisation of policies. Top management in the United Kingdom refers primarily to the directors of

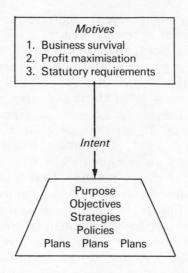

Figure 2.3   The hierarchy of business intent

companies as defined in the Companies Acts. Others may, of course, be involved in the preparation of policies but they would not be formally responsible for their adoption and review.

The expression of intent can best be seen in terms of corporate planning. This puts aside the daily preoccupations of operational management. It is concerned with the long run and how the business should be developed over such a time scale. Typically, this could cover a period of two to ten years. A shorter time scale encounters too many of the constraints of an ongoing business. Beyond ten years the setting usually becomes too tenuous for meaningful planning. This does not negate forecasting for longer ahead as a part of general business intelligence.

Corporate planning starts with the assessment of the business environment and how this might change with time. The environment is seen in economic, political, social and technological terms. The impact of expected changes, their nature and probability, are related to company operations. Thus a number of different scenarios is built up. Each has its structure, promise (plus or minus), likelihood; and to these can be added a proposed response. A portfolio of action alternatives is thus created in terms of established operations as well as new markets, products and processes. In the end a particular set of objectives is chosen and plans formulated for their attainment. It will be appreciated that corporate planning is an overall, integrated activity. It is more than a financial plan or an extrapolition of this year's budget; it embraces all the major functional areas of the business: marketing, manufacture, research and development, personnel and finance. It is concerned with all the resources required by the company to achieve its future objectives. This includes cash, trained personnel, equipment, processes and knowhow. Those who wish to know more about corporate planning are advised to consult such writers as Hertz[2] or Hussey[3].

The investment process and corporate planning

The comprehensive nature of corporate planning would be vitiated if the planning of future investments were excluded. This is particularly so where investments call for heavy financial commitments and where years may elapse before the plant comes into operational use — never mind the recovery of the initial outlay. Indeed, it is often the exigencies and costs of a proposed investment programme, with all its preconceptions and assumptions, which prompts some managements to look more carefully into the other functional constituents of corporate planning. For instance, a not uncommon experience is one where new production processes, embodied in recently installed equipment, call for a different labour and craft mix from what is currently available. Such a realisation emphasises the development and integration of all forward planning.

There are many links between corporate planning and the plant investment process. Indeed, the latter can be seen as a derivative of the former. There is a correlation between corporate planning and large-scale investment programmes. Both are characteristic of the big international corporation. In overall terms, the relationship between the two is illustrated by Figure 2.4. Simultaneous to the development of markets, products and processes of manufacture, attention is given to the planning of new production facilities. These include all production plant, services, land and buildings required to meet specified capacity targets. The plant investment process is one major form of implementing the corporate plan.

The impingement of the corporate plan is in the form of inputs to the three stages of the plant investment process. It begins with opportunity scanning and the whole catchment framework for stimuli, typically, in the Research and Development (R & D) function. It can govern the terms of reference set for project preparation and becomes an ingredient of project evaluation. At the decision stage the investment proposal is related to the corporate intent, which reappears after authorisation in the project brief.

It would be misleading, however, to suggest that corporate planning, whether explicit or intuitive, is the sole actuator of the plant investment process. As we shall see in Chapter 3, the stimuli, suggestions and pressures for plant investment can come from many quarters. Promising innovations and developments are not always perceived at the corporate level. Many minor schemes will be sustained by ongoing, delegated resources provisions; but above a given level the corporate intent must endorse and adopt them.

Investment and the organisation structure

Consider the number of plant projects authorised by a division of company B (engineering industry) in three successive years: 217, 257, 187; or for a factory of company D (food industry) for the same years: 238, 170, 89. The project value patterns approximate a Paretan distribution, i.e. a small number of projects account for a large percentage of the total investment value. The project numbers are sub-totals and are paralleled by other units in the respective companies. 81% of the projects for company B and 68% of the projects for company D were directly concerned with factory operations.

How should the work content of these projects be structured within a company organisation? The scrutiny of organisation charts — and many firms do not make their organisation explicit — suggests that only a modest number of companies make organisational provision for the preparation and implementation activities of the investment process. Both activities and responsibilities are scattered across the functional organisation. Such a situation is defended by reference to the intermittent and variable nature of investment projects within the company. Even where some organisational provision exists the groups concerned often have other briefs, such as production planning or process development. This is understandable. Yet something is lost and what this is can, perhaps, be best described as the initiative responsibility for the plant investment process. Consider Figures 2.5a and 2.5b. Each major function, such as marketing or production, has a senior executive responsible for its results. It is seldom that such a crystallised responsibility exists for a company's capital expenditure programme. Even where a works manager/director has a major involvement, his responsibilities are usually truncated. The differences in organisational treatment reflect some of the characteristics of the plant investment process. For instance, well-defined organisational roles reflect established operations; plant investment, as an agent of change, often runs counter to this. Large, strategic projects also involve other functions, apart from production. Figure 2.5b also suggests some more-detailed aspects which are often found with small/medium projects. It reflects the typical division of labour in an engineering firm in terms of routine operational activities. Plant investment studies do not come into such categories. We are concerned here with an amalgam of tech-

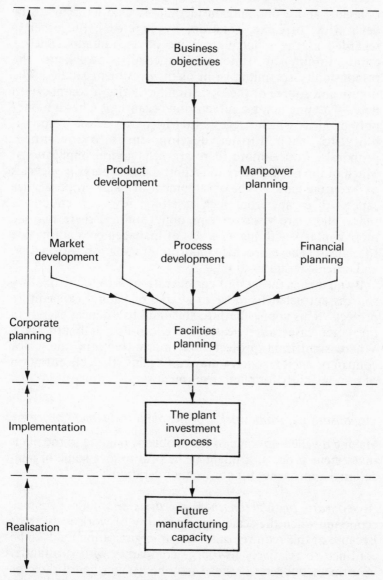

Figure 2.4 The plant investment process related to corporate planning

nological and economic considerations. One set tends to be dealt with, often in isolation, by engineers; the other is regarded as the usual prerogative of accountants. Such a condominium of functional specialists weakens the responsibility for initiative in plant investment studies. The nature and source of the first stimulus is also a complication here — no one in a manufacturing organisation has a monopoly of ideas which suggests that he be given sole responsibility for their further development into investment proposals. Furthermore there are behavioural implications. Much of the normal work at technical and supervisory level is of a routine nature. The development of plant proposals has aspects of escape from such a setting; however tenuous at times, there are vistas of new opportunities, there may be more contacts with higher levels of management and outside specialists. These provide opportunities for job satisfaction and other aspirations.

By no means the least of considerations is the control of resources entrusted to those in charge of capital expenditure projects. This applies both to staff and to finance, even if in the latter case cash releases are controlled at board level. Where significant projects are intermittent the quest for control of such resources may run against the concentration of responsibility for plant investment studies.

Organisational frameworks for the plant investment process

Having dwelled on some of the problems relating to the plant investment process, it might be helpful to give some organisational approaches for consistent operations:

A separate project/engineering division. This becomes economic when the scale and continuity of work is assured. Because of this requirement, such an organisation tends to be confined to relatively few large companies with substantial investment budgets. Its head may be a main board director and provide the link with corporate planning (where this exists) and policy levels. Such a division is normally

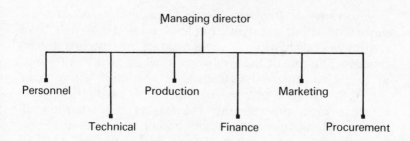

Figure 2.5 (a) Main functional divisions of a large engineering group

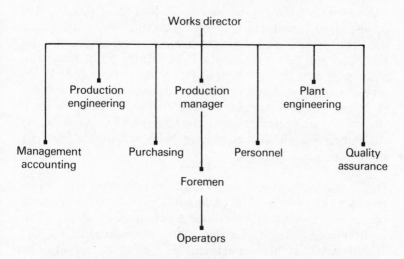

Figure 2.5 (b) Main sub-divisions of a typical engineering works organisation

responsible for most of the preparation and implementation stages of the plant investment process. Its relationships with operating divisions or factories are particularly important as these furnish much of the impetus and input for new projects as well as being in the 'client role'.

The specialist staff group. Where plant investments are at a more modest but still significant level a staff group may have special responsibilities for certain stages for the investment process. The role of the group has more of an advisory than an executive content. It reflects a staff function whose main job is to translate proposals from operating divisions into effective plant propositions, but leaving the execution of these to others. In a multi-factory organisation they are often a head office service department. Much of the work is assigned to major contractors and the group tends to become 'in-house' consulting engineers. Unless there are very severe fluctuations of capital expenditure, the group will have a permanent core and a wider membership which can vary by secondment of the appropriate specialists from, say, R & D or operating departments. If there is considerable variation in the type or size of individual projects then organisational flexibility will become important. Staff may be structured in a form of matrix organisation where they participate in an interdisciplinary project team, answerable to a project manager, yet still are responsible for specialist work to a specialist head of department. The nature and implications of such organisation structures have been well documented by such writers as Knight[4].

Direct line management responsibility. This approach can be found where much of a company's capital expenditure is composed of small to medium sized projects (say, up to £200000). In essence, the line manager responsible for the effectiveness of his department or works would also be responsible for the preparation and submission of investment proposals designed to improve its operations. He would be assisted by appropriate staff within his authority to whom the bulk of such tasks would be delegated. However, his responsibility would remain unabrogated. In a sense, he is both line and project manager.

Company A, for instance, regarded the formulation and handling of such matters as an aspect of managerial competence. It wanted its line managers to be involved and committed to project undertakings. They were also responsible for project execution, within authorised resources and a defined span of discretion. Line management involvement and responsibility for project preparation was seen to be fundamental, because those very same managers were subsequently expected to achieve the project intentions.

References

1. Urwick, L., *Elements of Administration,* Pitman, (London, 1947)
2. Hertz, D.B., *New Power for Management,* McGraw-Hill (New York, 1969)
3. Hussey, D.E., *Introducing Corporate Planning,* Pergamon Press, (Oxford, 1971)
4. Knight, K., *Matrix Management,* Gower Press, (Farnborough, Hants, 1977).

3 Investment and innovation

Because of the widely held belief that industrial progress, in terms of output and productivity, is largely governed by investment in new plant, it is appropriate to look for the operative factors in these investments which generate such progress.

Three aspects may be regarded as significant here. The first is investment in new plant, identical to that already installed, and increasing the total production capacity of a firm. This is the *'pure' expansion project*. The benefit here is often in terms of the economy of scale. The second is *'pure' plant replacement*, where ageing and deteriorating equipment is replaced by new identical units and a declining capacity is re-established. The third refers to investment in plant which embodies some *innovation*, normally the expression of technical change. In this chapter we are mainly concerned with this third aspect. It is of course appreciated that the segregation of these aspects is for the purpose of analysis only; in practice any mix is possible.

The meaning of innovation

In common usage the work 'innovation' is bedevilled by value judgements. To many, innovation implies progress — the direction of which may not always be clear — but as long as there is movement from a given existing state this is interpreted as desirable. However, we need to be more clinical about this term. For our purpose and in this context innovation may be described as the application of inventions to the process of production. In turn an invention consists of the creation of a new device, idea or technique. The invention can be a physical object, embodying technical change, such as a new type of fluidic switching device in a control system, or alternatively it could be in a disembodied form (i.e. without hardware) when it could be a new organisational technique, such as critical path analysis. The utilisation of a new invention by a manufacturing unit will affect its production situation and thus bring about innovation.

The stimulus for innovation

Whatever the form of innovation introduced by a firm, it can usually be related to some stimulus which makes the firm conscious of its substance and its promise. A business, like any other organisation, is susceptible to different stimuli, derived from its environmental setting. These stimuli may, typically, come from customers, competitors, trade unions, technical developments, etc. There is no obvious reason why such stimuli, which may affect different functional activities within the firm, need to be interrelated, particularly in the short run. They may be, but they do not have to be.

Consider a firm in a settled commercial position prior to the experience of a particular stimulus. Its sales are in balance with output, stock levels, costs and profits are in line with the normal trading experience of similar firms in the industry concerned. The stimulus may cause a reaction within the functional area of the firm concerned with it and much will depend subsequently on the receptivity and attitudes of the group of individuals involved. The character of the stimulus itself is of course an important variable. Where the stimulus is broad in impact, such as with changes in taxation or with investment incentives the reaction, whatever its form, may be swift, because the stimulus will normally come to the direct notice of the investment decision-making level. Similarly, where the stimulus is of such a magnitude that it is of immediate concern to those who control the business then again response may be quite rapid. An example of this might be the changing requirements of a major customer, affecting long-term bulk contracts. On the other hand, weaker stimuli or those not received at the investment decision-making level, are likely to elicit a much more variable response depending on the internal company situation. Some stimuli will be lost because of the 'friction effect' of a complex organisational system. They are hostage to organisational behaviour.

We are, of course, particularly concerned with the group of stimuli affecting the manner and rate of production. Again, the strength of these stimuli can be quite variable. For example, if it related to the details of a company's manufacturing process, observed but largely concealed by operating staff, the stimulus could be weak. Furthermore, if one were to relate the strength of a stimulus to the degree of perception and imagination required to see its implication for the firm as a whole, a great deal of such qualities would be needed to gather all the promising stimuli from the main stream of technological progress.

The stimulus for technical change may arise from the 'hearsay' of an industry: conferences, trade publications, exhibitions, etc. Both suppliers and customers exert an influence and where the latter is a substantial corporation with strong technological resources the influence could become commanding. Technical exchange agreements have grown in numbers, particularly where the cost of research and development work is high to the companies concerned.

The role of patents and licensing arrangements is also significant. Again, production problems have provided another well-known source of stimulus.

Perception here involves the relating of the new idea or development to the existing state of knowledge appropriate to the field in which the particular company operates. The knowledge itself can be divided into:

(i) *Established principles of working,* freely disseminated within the industry concerned. Ample illustrations from typical manufacturing tasks can be cited, such as metal cutting, forming or painting.

(ii) *Special or local knowledge* associated with a company's specific activities, not generally known or at times kept deliberately secret. Such knowledge comes closer to the art of manufacture rather than its science; it is often confined to a small number of individuals at technical or operating level, as distinct from the managerial level or the company as a whole, and there may be resistance to its formal definition (which would make it transferable) because of internal political or bargaining situations. Although tenuous, it exists.

When a new idea or stimulus is assessed this will involve a vision of its integration or application in a concrete form. Simultaneously an evaluation of possible risks or hazards may be associated with it. In a sense there is here a crude, near-subconscious cost benefit analysis or a 'take further/ leave alone' mechanism. Again, these initial decision processes are exposed to social and group influences, the nature of motivation and the degree of integration of the individuals concerned with the objectives and policies of the company.

The precise nature of the risks involved is in part a function of technical variables. With the continuous growth of technical knowledge and the attendant specialisation at advanced level, more and more of the necessary problem solving requires the coordination of specialists. This in turn affects the manner of approach and the organisational framework within which the problem solving and implementation

Table 3.1 Functional source distribution of stimuli leading
to research projects %

	Research	*Operating unit*	*Sales*	*Others*
UK companies	45	26	16	18
USA companies	50	15	25	10

work is carried out. Studies by Woodward[1] and Burns and
Stalker[2] indicate an association between a high degree of technical change and the use of committees as an organisational
instrument to handle such changes. The company's
organisation structure, particularly in those areas closely
associated with technical change, such as with research and
development or prototype manufacture, becomes more
'organic'. This reflects a response to the opportunities of
technical change. The transformation of technical
opportunities into investment propositions is also often
handled within a different organisational framework.
Furthermore, the technical problems, if capable of solution
with a given overall state of knowledge in the fields
concerned, may determine the timetable for investment
proposals.

Let us now revert to the company's general position. Many
of the minor stimuli which it encounters at various levels may
eventually result in product improvements and/or refinements in manufacturing techniques. Within a given state of
technology these may tend to reduce manufacturing costs in
real terms. Taking any one of these changes on its own, it is
unlikely to make a profound impact on the firm's competitive
position. However, the cumulative effects of continuous,
even if small, changes cannot be ignored. Lower costs will
increase the company's profits in a given market situation.
Alternatively the firm will be able to reduce its prices or
furnish a superior product. In this manner it is able to
increase its market share. A similar change could also occur
with a major technical development and although the overall
time scale could, but need not, be as long, the economic

effects, once the change has been successfully achieved, are often more drastic. In both cases it has been presumed that returns to scale are constant; if there are increasing returns with a greater volume of output, the corresponding gain will be the greater.

The sources of stimuli

A firm which wants to harness stimuli leading to innovation and improvement is likely to look at its information system — formal and informal — to discover the more promising sources. How should the antennae be arranged; how should the intelligence be picked up and evaluated?

Where and how does the innovation process begin within the different functional departments of a 'typical' manufacturing company? In what area, as distinct from organisational level, is the original stimulus? The main problem is one of systematic and accurate observation. It must be remembered that there could be a long time scale between an observer's awareness of an original phenomenon and his perception of an opportunity relating to it. Furthermore there is also the position of the observer himself within the organisation and his assessment of the phenomena concerned.

Nevertheless, provided the limitations in accuracy are appreciated a broad analysis can be made. An interesting example was furnished some years ago by Carter and Williams[3] who broadly apportioned stimuli as sources of research projects into the functional areas shown in Table 3.1. Because of problems of detailed classification these figures are best regarded as indicative. Nevertheless, they show interesting differences between the two countries in the contribution of stimuli from the manufacturing and marketing functions. One can differentiate between the innovations from such different functional source areas. Thus, innovation, based on the perception of wants of potential customers, may be primarily the application of existing technical and operating knowledge to new opportunities. Such an opportunity is external to the firm; on the other hand, stimuli from operating units often reflect opportunities from within which lead to greater specialist knowledge, embodied in improved manufacturing processes.

The link between investment and innovation

As we shall see in more detail in Chapter 5, the economic worth of a plant investment proposal is obtained by the comparison between capital expenditure now and revenue benefits to come. The expected benefits have two main sources. They come either from extra contributions due to expansion or from cost reduction. A given set of project benefits can, of course, draw from both categories, say, in the form of greater output and reduced direct costs. Cost reduction usually entails a change in manufacturing activities. This change need not always have a significant plant investment content. For instance, industrial engineering techniques, such as method study or value analysis, can lead to greater productivity and achieve important cost reductions. But however significant such contributions might be they are normally encapsulated within and limited by a given state of technology. Sooner or later changes in manufacturing processes need different equipment; a plant investment is required. Thus, the first link between investment and innovation is that the former is a major agent for implementing the latter.

The second link is concerned with the constituent stages of the plant investment process. As we shall see in Chapter 4, when a major change in production methods is contemplated much of the necessary technical work will be carried out during the project preparation and implementation stages. New designs have still to be proven or prototypes will have to be transcribed into production units. These later stages of development work, i.e. the innovative task, might not be carried through if there were no intention to invest. Thus, there can be a substantial innovation work content in the

Technical/development work as a project cost constituent		Type of project
%	Grading	
100	Total	Pure R & D project No plant investment
75 50 25	Predominant Substantial Significant	Composite projects
0	Zero	No preparation work 'shopping basket' plant investment

Figure 3.1 The technical/development content of plant investment projects

plant investment process itself. Of course, this task component can be extremely variable and Figure 3.1 gives some indication of its range, which can be translated into cost terms. At one end of the scale we have 'pure' research and development projects which call for no new equipment. As far as process improvements are concerned, this is not very common; it may be more likely with product research. At the other end of the scale there is the simple purchase of new production equipment with no preparatory or development work involved. Where this occurs it is often a repeat investment where the technical task component of a previous plant investment is spread over subsequent acquisitions. This is also more the case with expansion rather than cost reduction projects.

Many plant schemes, however, fall between these two extremes and can therefore be regarded as composite projects. They involve some measure of technical change and emphasise the link between investment and innovation. This connection will now be further explored with particular reference to the nature of production.

The production setting

Consider the production processes used by a manufacturing business. In the simplest context the manufacturing task consists of what is technologically one process. This was typified by what once was the traditional division of labour within the Lancashire cotton industry when separate firms concentrated on one of each of the main industrial processes, carding, spinning, weaving and finishing. However, in many modern manufacturing industries, typically engineering, aircraft and vehicle building, manufacturing processes may be numerous and complex. It is commonplace here to find, for instance, that the manufacture of parts and the assembly of the final product involves a number of discrete operations in functionally and organisationally separate sections of the firm. The output of one process area serves as an input to the next one in the process. Each department may have its own specialists engaged in a specific technology which has its own fund of knowledge and experience as well as specialist equipment which physically incorporates it. Its practitioners receive specialised training and may spend their whole working life in their chosen field. Much of their skill and experience has limited value in other technological areas; transferability is thus limited. To a considerable extent a specialised technology can develop in isolation from others; there could, but need not, be a correlation between the developments within different technologies. For instance, in the motor industry there is no immediate technical connection between the development of paint technology for car body protection and welding technology for high-speed body assembly work. Both technologies are closely concerned with car body manufacture but, in terms of specialist knowledge, prospective developments and equipment, they are quite distinct.

For the purpose of analysis it is therefore helpful to see manufacture in multi-technological terms. Schematically this is illustrated by Figure 3.2.

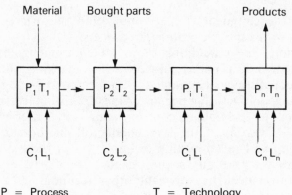

P = Process   T = Technology
C = Capital input   L = Labour input

Figure 3.2   Schematic concept of a manufacturing unit
having 'n' processes and technologies

We can say, as a simplification, that a firm uses 'n' distinct production processes involving 'n' technologies. Each technology is embodied in its own type of equipment. This determines the level of equipment contribution 'C' to the production task as well as the labour content 'L' of the operation. In economic theory this reflects the concept of the production function where, with a given technology, a specified output requires corresponding inputs of capital and labour. A high value of 'C' combined with a low level of 'L' per unit of output suggests a capital-intensive process with 'L' approaching zero as the process becomes fully automated. Conversely, a high value of 'L' with a low level of 'C' indicates a labour-intensive process. The C/L mix is a function of technology and costs and can show wide fluctuations for different processes within one factory.

The length of the technology chain can vary substantially between industries or even between factories in a given industry. The chain is time-sensitive, depending on the pattern of industrial innovation. Of course, some processes may be regarded as more important than others; indeed, at any given period one process may be crucial. However, this does not make the rest negligible.

A further development is the combination of different technologies with a specific production process.

For example, the machining of metal components by computer controlled or numerically controlled machine tools involves several distinct technologies, with their contributions fused for one manufacturing purpose. One can distinguish in this case computer technology, control engineering, materials technology (in respect of the semi-conductors in the electronic circuits) and metal cutting technology. All these are quite distinct yet relevant to the purpose. Similarly, the advent of automation has brought other technologies to many production processes in different fields of manufacture.

Technical change

Using the concept of the multi-technology approach, innovation, brought about by investment, will affect the chain of technologies used by the industrial company. The purpose of this section is to explore some of the implications of such a process. However, before embarking on this it would be helpful to consider further the meaning of technical change. It is even better to go back to the very term: technology.

There is no universally agreed meaning to the word 'technology'; none of the simplicity or clarity of a mathematical term or physical constant. We are driven to the common usage of language, to the dictionaries. One of the uses of the word stated in the *Oxford English Dictionary* is taken here: 'Technology is the scientific study of the practical or industrial arts'. The definition has the disadvantage of imprecision which stems from its historical pattern of usage. It remains a limited and somewhat blunt tool. Also, it follows from such a definition that an enquiry into technology is a second-order study in so far as it is an analysis of a study itself. The first-order study, i.e. technology, is concerned with the industrial arts; it uses scientific method in areas which have not completely yielded to scientific enquiry. The 'art' element reflected in craft know-how is still of importance in some industries.

The etymological references to technology in the *Oxford English Dictionary* are of the seventeenth, eighteenth and nineteenth centuries. Phillips, (ed. Kersey) 1706, refers to technology in his dictionary as a description of the Arts, *especially the Mechanical.* Subsequent references widen the use of the term technology but these do not go beyond 1882. Considering the profound changes that have taken place since, the lack of more recent references is significant. The yield of scientific progress since 1882 and its effects on 'industrial arts' is inadequately reflected. The definition implies the prior existence of these arts which are then subject to scientific scrutiny. Many of the current technologies (atomic power generation, the manufacture of petro-chemicals, etc.) are the derivatives, the projection of scientific developments: 'industrial arts' followed the scientific enquiries here, they did not precede them.

Notwithstanding all these difficulties, the scientific approach to the study of technology is worthwhile provided the difficulties in its way are appreciated. The preoccupation with definition illustrates also some of the problems of description of what is to come.

Returning to the concept of technical change, it would follow from the adopted use of the word 'technology' that it is the change of these 'practical or industrial arts' with which we are concerned when we speak of technical change. There is nothing, however, in this interpretation which suggests how such changes come about; whether they are due to small refinements of working practice, which could well include an element of practical art, or whether they are the result of the successful application of new scientific discoveries. Furthermore, it is conceded that such interpretation, although meaningful, somewhat lacks impact or, for that matter, elegance, and one can sympathise with the economic theorist who prefers the description of effect to the analysis of the substance.

It is a matter of experience that technical change varies substantially with time. Also, its effects on different industries can be quite varied. This is particularly so with embodied technological change, i.e. the change which is expressed in new or modified production plant. It is this type of variability which has given rise to the term 'technological period'. The concept of a technological period is perhaps best illustrated by a diagram.

A technological epoch is one of the near-flat sections of the curve in Figure 3.3. It is governed by the prevailing level of technology embodied in current plant and equipment. The section is not quite flat because, even with a given generation of equipment, refinement and improvements are possible. But there are diminishing returns with this as the practical boundaries of a technology are reached. The plateau continues until innovations introduce the next generation of equipment. A relatively short period of rapid technical change then occurs which is reflected in a considerable improvement of a key aspect, such as the speed of an aircraft, the efficiency of power generation or the rate of output of a manufacturing unit.

Normally a company can move from one to the next generation of equipment only by replacing its obsolete plant. For this an investment programme will be needed. A company will require appropriate finance and staff resources to make this transition; otherwise it will stay at the lower level of technology, with all that this implies. Essentially, technical change prompts or even forces investment and re-investment. The rate of response by industrial companies to embodied technical change depends of course also on such aspects as the profitabilty of the consequent investments, finance and market conditions. These affect the time scale of transition but do not avoid the need to make the change (we are assuming the context of an advanced industrial economy). The nature of this response rate, seen as a time function of investment, has been studied by Mansfield[4] who suggests that the pattern of transition within an industry approximates an 'S' curve.

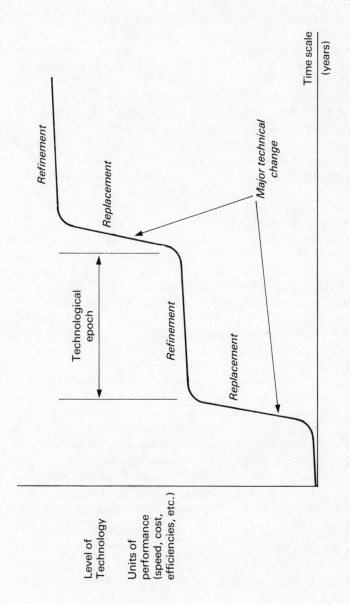

Figure 3.3   The concept of a technological epoch

The interaction effects of technical change

After considering the meaning and nature of technical change it is helpful to review some of its possible effects in a given manufacturing situation.

It is a matter of common observation that some manufacturing firms use relatively few technological processes while others use a wide spectrum. Typically, a firm will have its own technologies of manufacture and these will be associated with the technologies embodied in its equipment. In a practical sense it is now inconceivable that a firm is only involved with one technology because there is little production plant which does not itself embody a number of different technologies. It is therefore meaningful to view a manufacturing firm as one which uses a number of different technologies, each at a different stage of evolution and also changing at different rates. It is also accepted that some of these technologies are more important to the firm than others. This would be a function of the firm's product and manufacturing objectives as well as its cost spectrum.

Consider a manufacturing situation where a number of distinct processes are used, involving a corresponding number of different technologies. Let one or several of these processes be affected by technological change. This change can either be direct, affecting the process concerned, or indirect, where the process basically remains unaltered, but its manipulation is affected, such as with a system of automatic control. Furthermore, the economic prospect of such a change could either be so significant that in a competitive situation the firm is quickly forced to replace its obsolete plant in order to stay in business or alternatively, in a less pressing context, it can associate the technological change with its routine plant replacement policies. These various aspects of technical change could have the following effects:

'Zero interaction'. The technical change in respect of one or more processes has no effect whatsoever on any of the other processes. In economic terms therefore its justification will be

found within the process situation itself. Such a situation is only likely to arise when a particular process is completely self-contained.

'Capacity imbalance'. This can occur when as a result of technical change one of a number of discrete process units acquires a much larger capacity rate than the remainder. To balance its production flow the firm will either have to run the unit concerned below its full utilisation rate or, in the absence of technical change for the other processes, invest in more plant. Either solution could reduce the potential benefit indicated by the technical change and much will depend on the yield of further plant investment in deciding which alternative to pursue. If the company has flexibility in the use of shift work or systematic overtime a short-term balance could be achieved, particularly where the prospect of technological changes will further affect the capacity equilibrium.

'The residual process problem'. In this case the technological transformation of one or several processes constitutes such a profound change that a severe imbalance of manufacturing activities could occur. The unchanged production processes may become a bottleneck and induce the firm to make such processes the focus of its research and development activities.

'Secondary process effects'. These are the minor influences of technical change in one process area which affect but do not radically alter working practices in other areas. A typical example of this is the range of impurities in chemical feed-stocks which have been derived from alternative process routes. Operating practices, such as the control of reactions, may have to be modified; a change in the technique of working has to be accommodated. This does not by itself involve technological change. Nevertheless if working practices are not altered there could be a cumulative effect on efficiencies or operating costs. Such fringe effects may influence quality control at subsequent process stages; they could simplify or complicate quality control problems.

'The process fusion effect'. This is often the result of indirect technological change, typically a consequence of automation, where formerly discrete production processes are so integrated within a system of control that they become, in essence, one continuous production process. Such developments are well known in the chemical and petro-chemical industries and may also be noted in the metal industries with the introduction of 'machining centres'.

The measurement of technical change at plant level

There is relatively little published material on this subject and scarcely any reports of systematic empirical investigations. Mansfield[5], in a study of research on innovation, cites a subjective assessment technique to evaluate the extent of technical change. In his reported investigation experienced project administrators and scientists were asked to rate the magnitude of improvement in the 'state of the art' contained in a group of projects. A top score of 5.0 meant very much improvement; at the other end of the scale a score of 1.0 indicated no improvement. The score for each project was obtained from the mean of all respondent ratings. This form of rating scale is a relatively blunt tool and consistency of judgement could be a difficulty when making inter-firm or inter-industry comparisons. Nevertheless, the approach is significant as it introduces into the assessment of technical change a component of scientific and specialist judgement, rather than confining the evaluation to economic consequences.

Rothwell[6] in a study of the relationships between technical change and economic performance in the mechanical engineering industry uses such indicators as value/weight ratios and unit equipment values. These are seen as indicators of equipment sophistication. Changes in these indicators are presumed to reflect technical change to some extent.

The more conventional economic view has been well stated by Salter[7]. Technical change from one period to another is measured by the relative change in total unit costs when the techniques in each period are those which would minimise unit costs and when factor prices are held constant. Salter's view is based on the scrutiny of published industrial statistics — not on intra-firm analysis. A number of alternative measurements have been suggested, typically, based on changes of output per manhour. This form of index, however, is impaired when it is related only to labour input.

In the subsequent analysis a slightly more refined assessment technique for technical change is proposed. It is a ranking method which, in addition to the conventional economic factor ratios, considers the 'upheaval' brought about by the change. Upheaval refers here to the physical changes that occur in the production situation and in the manner in which production is carried out. Such changes require managerial effort and thus reflect organisational factors relevant to the rate of technical change within the firm. The following factors are taken into account in the development of Table 3.2:

(i) Changes in output.
(ii) The labour input in total and per unit of output.
(iii) The total capital employed as well as the capital per unit of output.
(iv) The sequence and manner of work as expressed in a flow process chart form.
(v) The physical changes in equipment, plant structures, tooling, layout.
(vi) The manner of work or process control and the general flow of work in progress.
(vii) Changes in materials and materials utilisation.

The development of such a scale for the evaluation of technical change is somewhat artificial; subjective judgement is not eliminated. However, a limited technique in an area where few exist may nevertheless justify itself and because of this the attempt is made. The difficulties are recognised. Nonetheless, the writer has been able to apply it and obtain useful inter-firm comparisons.

Some general effects of innovation on production

With a given production plant and product specification the most frequent change is an increase in the rate of output. A further major effect of embodied innovation is the reduction in the labour content of the production task. For instance, in a sample of twenty projects with significant technical change, examined by the writer, seventeen projects showed such a reduction.

There can also be qualitative changes in the manufactured product, i.e. innovation may alter the product specification. Greater quality with a given cost/price structure affects the product demand pattern and the firm may reap the expected project benefit from perceived market opportunities. Of course, any combination of quantitative and qualitative change is possible, although in practice there often is a polarisation towards one form of change with a given investment proposal. A typical example of composite change can be observed where the main investment purpose is the expansion of production capacity, and the installation of new equipment brings about an improvement in product quality. It may also be appropriate here to consider some physical consequences resulting from innovation. For simplicity these can be categorised as follows:

Existing equipment — change in manner of use. A change in working practice could be a function of technical and organisational change. It can involve minor investment commitments, such as the purchase of tools or accessories. The cost of making a change here could be, say, 10% investment in new working tools, 90% in staff time to develop, refine and to implement a change in the manner of plant use. The significant factor may not be the cost relationships, but the input of various organisational resources. Their availability may matter more, rather than their costs, particularly where a business can use such resources economically and its overhead burden already reflects this.

Table 3.2   An ordinal scale of technical change for
production plant

Ranking	Degree of change	Interpretation
0	No change	No technical change, e.g. an identical replacement or addition.
1	Marginal	A minor or detail technical change with no operational significance.
2	Refinement	A minor or detail technical change with a slight operational significance. The benefit accruing from such a change is regarded as insufficient to stop ongoing operations. The change is likely to be incorporated at a suitable opportunity, such as a plant overhaul or the annual plant shutdown.
3	Noticeable	A group of minor technical changes of rank 2 which become more significant by summation. Operator guidance is required to achieve familiarisation with the changed process or plant features.
4	Considerable	A significant change with definite operational implications. The change will be adopted as quickly as practicable in the operating context. The main process and plant however remain the same. Operator instruction/training will be required and the grade of labour used may be affected.
5	Important	A group of changes of rank 4.
6	Substantial	A major change affecting production plant or processes including plant structure, control and operation. Equipment not incorporating such a change will be retired as obsolescent.
7	Extensive	A group of changes of rank 6.
8	Complete	An entirely different process and plant.

Existing equipment — physical rearrangement. Here the change may reflect physical alteration in the plant layout which may or may not alter the sequence of production operations. In such a case the physical changes could significantly affect the production situation, particularly in relation to costs and possible interference with the actual production process. The pre-planning of such a change involves considerable staff resources. The success of such a change, as might also be the case with the category described above, could depend not only on the extent to which staff resources are available but also on their level of skill and attainment, which in turn could be a function of the educational level of technological manpower.

Investment in new production plant. Here the change in the production situation is primarily the result of the acquisition by the business of further equipment. The introduction of additional production plant may be a specific change in itself; however it could also bring about changes under the first two categories. Thus, for instance, the equilibrium of plant use may be affected and this could be irrespective of whether the acquired equipment is new and brings with it a change in the technology of production. Neither is it necessary for the introduced equipment to be new in a commercial sense.

Innovation and cost reduction

In the context of embodied technical change the relationship between innovation and investment is well known. But precisely how does such a relationship come about? In the normal way investment projects, which are justified on economic grounds, stand or fall on the incremental benefits they promise. Such benefits are accounted for either by more money being received or less money being spent. Naturally, a combination of the two is also possible. Usually an increase in receipts reflects an expansion project whilst a saving is the reason for the cost reduction project. The use of these two expressions suggests a polarisation of capital projects in terms of their justification benefits.

A study of the practice of industrial project preparation and authorisation strongly suggests that the pattern of stated benefits is not a random one. Organisational and behavioural factors have a bearing on it. The organisational structure of anything but the smallest firm reflects some form of functional specialisation. Some individuals or groups will concentrate, by virtue of their role specification, on special aspects of the company's activities, such as market exploration or the improvement of production processes. Also, the larger the firm, the greater will be the tendency to functional specialisation within its organisational structure.

A particular instance of this is the industrial research and development department which is a major, but not the sole, instrument of technical change. Typically, the organisational framework is that of the larger corporation which has appropriate financial and technical resources. It must also be remembered that there is a relationship between the size of an organisation and the pattern of information flow within it. The more levels of authority and/or the more functional specialisation, the greater is the problem of integrating these specialist contributions. The proponents and exponents of a new project thus tend to come from the same functional area. This is particularly so with small- and medium-sized projects, say below £200000 (1978 prices) which are more of departmental interest. An alert and systematic management would, of course, satisfy itself that the project implications for non-originating functional areas would also be examined. But this is more of a checking activity than a partnership in initiative.

Given that there is a diversity in the functional origin and justification of capital projects, one would expect a given project to reflect some of the expectations of the sponsoring department. Thus straight expansion projects could emanate from production, coupled with marketing support, while cost reduction proposals would tend to originate from the departments which have a formal responsibility for such work. Furthermore, there is no obvious reason why market opportunities should coincide with particular process developments, except as the result of the latter. So it is quite plausible that, with an ongoing concern, projects could be mainly of one type or other rather than be of the composite form. Apart from the special case of the 'strategic' project, which is so substantial that it encompasses all the functional areas of the firm, this seems largely to be the case.

A pilot study by the author of thirty projects with the four mentioned companies showed twenty-six with strong benefit polarisation. For twelve of these projects the benefits were predominantly due to expansion; for the other fourteen they were due essentially to cost reduction, with expansion, if any, at most an incidental advantage. Applying the scale for technical change as per Table 3.2, cost reduction projects achieved much higher ranking values than straight expansion schemes. This supports the view that there is a strong link between technical change and cost reduction.

References

1. Woodward, J., *Industrial Organisation: Theory and Practice,* Oxford University Press (Oxford, 1965)
2. Burns, T. and Stalker, G.M., *The Management of Innovation,* Tavistock, (London, 1961)
3. Carter, C.F. and Williams, B.R., *Industry and Technical Progress,* Oxford University Press (Oxford, 1957)
4. Mansfield, E., *Technical Change and the Rate of Imitation,* Econometrica, *29,* 741, Oct. 1961
5. Mansfield, E., et al., *Research and Innovation in the Modern Corporation,* MacMillan (London, 1972)
6. Rothwell, R., *The Relationship between Technical Change and Economic Performance in Mechanical Engineering: Some Evidence,* International Symposium on Industrial Innovation, University of Strathclyde, September 1977
7. Salter, W.E.G., *Productivity and Technical Change,* Cambridge University Press (Cambridge, 1969)

4   Project preparation

We have seen in Chapter 2 that the project preparation phase is the first major stage of the plant investment process. First in sequence, it has profound implications for what follows; the project preparation stage sows the seeds of success, mischief or disaster.

The project preparation stage embraces all the activities between the moment of 'stimulus response' and the presentation of a definitive proposal for authorisation. The three main sub-sections of this stage consist of:

1. Feasibility analysis.
2. Authorisation of project development resources.
3. Project development and definition.

One can expect to find these stages for every project above a certain size (say, £250000 at 1978 prices) and also for many below such level. It will be noted from Figures 4.1-3 that each section can comprise quite a number of activities. Depending on the project, these need not all be carried out within the company. Management consultants, consulting engineers or, in some industries, prospective main contractors may participate in this work. Obviously, there will be many small projects where some of the indicated task components will not be needed. For instance, a straightforward, but minor, expansion project may require little more of the project preparation stage than proposal definition. All the basic information is already available and its collation requires little time and effort. However, a cost reduction project involving technical change may encompass all stages. In principle, the totality of the project preparation stage depends on the complexity of the evolving proposition.

Feasibility analysis

As we can see from Figure 4.1 the input to this part of the project preparation system consists of stimuli — ideas of all sorts. They come from many quarters, both from within and outside the firm. They can be at random or be encouraged by management such as through suggestion schemes, brainstorming sessions, value analysis, lateral thinking and similar techniques. The catchment of stimuli, the establishment of ideas portfolios — this is the first opportunity within the investment process for an alert management. Needless to say, the 'climate' of the company, its organisational behaviour, governs the success of such intentions.

When a firm visualises an investment opportunity in new production plant we imply an opportunity awareness at an appropriate decision-making level. This is either at a level of authority at which decisions about commensurate company resources can be made or, alternatively, at an immediately subordinate level whose proposals are normally given serious consideration by the first group. Such an interpretation will therefore rule out the investment idea or opportunity awareness, however promising, which is possessed by an employee, who is at a level substantially below the appropriate decision level in the company hierarchy. Only when the ideas reach such a level can they be considered. This may be significant in the context of a firm's information system; whatever stimulus reaches the decision-making level, whether by intent or chance, is likely to obtain speedier attention than the stimuli which first have to be absorbed and

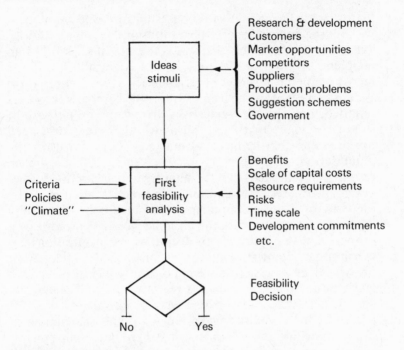

Figure 4.1   The concept of feasibility analysis

transcribed by such a system.

Let us now presume that the opportunity is perceived at the appropriate level — what happens? Perception is a mental recognition by one or more individuals of the existence and suggested implications of an opportunity. The implications need to be meaningful to those concerned in terms of criteria by which their affairs are judged. Such implications may be expressed in terms of profit, sales, productivity, quality, etc., and possibly a whole host of other considerations which seem relevant to those involved. The opportunity may be described in a crude form of proposition which embodies the insight or reflection following perception. The proposition is crude in the sense that no organisational resources have been applied to its definition or validation. (This excludes the possibility that a particular executive espouses an idea and develops it without the knowledge of his organisation.)

Essentially, feasibility analysis is the first inspection of an incipient proposition. It endeavours to establish: (i) the merits of the proposition in terms of the chosen criteria, (ii) the costs expected to be incurred; (iii) the company resources required, and (iv) the likely risks involved. The purpose of this first view is to establish whether the envisaged opportunity should have formal recognition within the organisation. If the proposition *is* given such a status then resources, if needed, can be allocated to it for its further development. Such recognition is in practice often given by the issue of a project number or accounts code. Feasibility analysis does not confirm the ultimate worth or promise of a proposition. All it does is to decide which propositions are worth some organisational support for further consideration; or, where the inverse is more important, which proposals to leave alone. Where so much is tentative the judgements are largely subjective even on relatively technical matters. The nature of the organisational framework and the climate of expectations are important and it is here that well-thought-out policies provide a helpful setting for the first stage of decision making.

The initial feasibility study is usually, but not necessarily, carried out by the functional department which responded to the original stimulus. Informal discussions with other interested departments may, of course, be included in this. For instance, a growing factory work load may prompt a production manager to consider a plant extension. Initial discussions with marketing would seek to establish the permanence of current market trends. There is some expectation by the initiating department that it would have operational control of the proposed capital equipment. This would not happen in every case, but where feasibility is confirmed, a chaperon for the proposition usually emerges and it is appropriate that it should be those concerned with the operational realisation of the proposal.

The actual mechanics of a first appraisal are often

informal, such as the 'back of the envelope' calculation. It is, however, relatively easy to put feasibility analysis on a systematic basis. An idea usually has an exponent or sponsor. He can enter on a simple form a description of the idea, its purpose, prospects and problems. To the first analysis can also be added a 'second opinion' — someone sufficiently apart from the proposal to have no prior views could act as an auditor. This is particularly valuable where a plant proposition has a significant development/design content. This type of approach is common with suggestion schemes and can be applied to other situations.

The marshalling and tentative evaluation of all relevant data provides the setting for the feasibility decision. The main proposition elements (capital costs, revenue benefits, risks and implications) are related to given criteria and policies. The decision often combines economic and technical judgement. The decision may be made by the functional manager concerned or sometimes by a technical committee responsible for such first-stage decisions.

If the proposal has survived this first hurdle, it will pass to the next section of the preparation system.

The authorisation of project resources

The proposal, designated as 'feasible', enters the next struggle for survival. It is now formally recognised and quickly becomes a claimant of resources. Subsequent growth and success is a function of the resources it will be able to obtain. In this respect, proposal needs are variable and have to be matched with what can be supplied. Our 'infant' project is usually in competition with other claimants.

The resources consists primarily of managerial and technical staff capable of developing, shaping and refining a capital expenditure proposition. Of course, other resources are also needed; for instance, in a process or plant development situation these could, typically, include equipment and materials. However, the quantity and quality of the available specialist resources remain the key to progress at this stage. These resources can be augmented; additional staff can be recruited and trained. But there is a limit to this, particularly in the short run. The supply of some specialists is relatively inelastic and the time-lag before a firm receives an effective contribution from such extra staff can be considerable. Also, management may be hesitant about violent swings in such staff resources. Alternatives, such as the contracting-out of certain preparation tasks, typically routine draughting work, may be possible to a limited extent. Similarly, the technical staff of a consultant or a would-be contractor may be used. The need, however, for such additional resources is greatest where the project has a large development content — and these are the very cases where outside assistance is less suitable.

The main constituents of the project resources authorisation process are shown in Figure 4.2. These presume the more complex project situation where the scale, mix and technical content of the prospective project call for systematic definition and computation of manpower requirements. Typically, this is a large composite project with a strong design/development content. It must be remembered that only project preparation resources are involved. Where the scale and complexity of a project are more modest, informal, short-cut methods will be common. Nevertheless, in principle, these stages occur, even if they are reduced to an intuitive level.

Proposal feasibility can be taken to mean that on first view the proposal holds sufficient promise to warrant further development. In essence, there is a basic credibility about the idea. However, there is no certainty about its success. One of the tasks of project preparation is to study the implications of the proposal, particularly the major problems. Preparation work is as much risk reduction as proposition crystallisation.

Proposal resources definition. Resources definition for project preparation is, then, primarily concerned with the

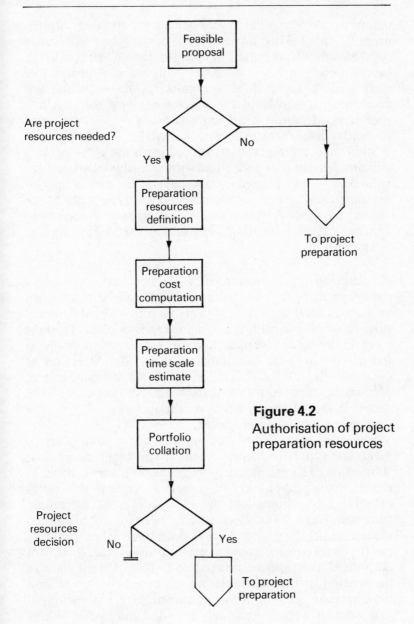

Figure 4.2
Authorisation of project
preparation resources

manpower requirements to generate a meaningful investment proposition. Taking an example, this might read: thirty men/month for mechanical design, ten men/month for model prototype work, etc., etc. A measure of prospective staff loading would thus be obtained. Such a preliminary assessment is similar to the process of shop loading in a production department where the capacity requirements of a particular job have to be established for scheduling and machine allocation purposes. Indeed, with the growing costs and problems of hiring staff and subsequently declaring them redundant — only to need them again, say, six months later — certain groups of key technologists may acquire some of the characteristics of 'fixed assets' calling for much more systematic work estimating and planning to ensure economic operations.

Preparation cost computation. Once basic resource requirements have been estimated these can be transcribed into costs. Staff time requirements multiplied by the appropriate cost rates furnish the initial manpower costs. To these have to be added supporting project expenses such as materials. The basis of computation and the allocation of overheads depend, of course, on the system of management accounting operated by the firm. Whatever that might be in detail, it should clearly delineate the incremental cost of a particular proposal development.

It must be remembered that the costs of proposal development are generally incorporated in the plant investment submission. The expenditure, so to speak, is on account, in the hope and expectation of project success. If this yields effective production plant the expense may be capitalised retrospectively. (Taxation aspects need to be examined separately.) If the proposal development gets into difficulties or the subsequent capital expenditure request is not authorised, the expense incurred up to that date will have to be written off if sizeable or absorbed by a general development account. It is presumed here that proposal development work is separately recorded and costed. Where costs are likely to be small they may be absorbed within departmental budgets.

Time scale definition. It is now possible to furnish a preparation resources and cost estimate together with a time scale for proposal submission. This is input information for the scheduling of technical manpower and for the resources authorisation decision. The time scale can also be significant for development cost cash-flow reasons. It further indicates when the main investment decision can be taken. In a competitive situation the timing of that decision could be important.

Proposal portfolio collation. With a substantial company a number of feasible proposals can emerge in a given period. Within an established system they are all subject to the same evaluation process. Now they are assembled for project resources authorisation. Collation here is more than mere listing because of possible proposal interaction effects. The periodic portfolio decision approach gives a better overview and facilitates the integration of subsequent investment proposal development. Alternatively, decisions can be made on individual proposals as they emerge.

The resources authorisation decision. As already indicated, the resources authorisation decision is concerned with those composite plant investment opportunities which make substantial calls on preparatory resources. It settles to which opportunities the available resources shall be applied. Calls are matched with available or prospective resources and ongoing commitments. Proposals which require none or so little that they can be accommodated by the 'organisational slack' (extra built-in work capacity) bypass the whole of this module and proceed to the preparation task. The decision process becomes similar to those used for selecting research and development projects. These have been well documented by Beattie and Reader[1]. Some of the economic decision aspects will be discussed in the next section. At this stage it should be remembered that projects can be considered individually or in clusters, that schedules may be specified for the supported projects and that a 'no' may only be until the next review period. Policy considerations, such as the use of 'know-how' and technical exchange agreements with other firms, can also be important considerations here.

The decisions are often made by formal or informal technical or management committees chaired or guided by a board member particularly concerned with corporate plans.

Project development and definition

We come now to the core of the project preparation process. It will be seen from Figure 4.3 that this consists of four modules: Preparation planning, Detailed functional analysis, Functional development and Proposal definition. This is the full model which incorporates the special aspects of an investment proposal associated with development and technical change. Again, for simpler cases the modules will be reduced in number and content.

Preparation planning

The preparation planning stage applies where the project preparation task is substantial and/or complex. The nature of the operation requires definition of what is to be done, by whom and by what date. Preparation planning is comparable in structure to project-planning. The difference is in the objectives. The latter is normally concerned with tangible results — typically, new machines, processes or buildings — here, the end product is a document, a proposition. Yet the proposition, to be credible, has to anticipate and simulate these physical developments.

The first task is a more detailed specification of intent. To some extent this may already have been anticipated at the feasibility analysis and resources authorisation stages. The basic

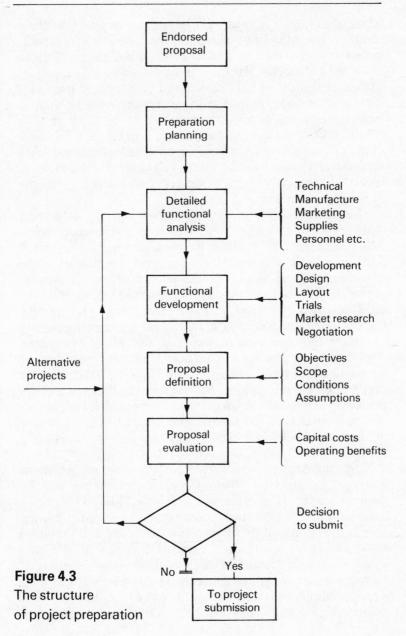

Figure 4.3
The structure
of project preparation

terms of reference may already be there. For example, these could be: prepare within six months the specification and estimate for a new factory in Brazil, given the choice of three alternative capacity levels or product mixes. Or, submit within three months fully costed and documented proposals for a machine line running at three very different alternative speeds. The more detailed statement of intent is designed to furnish a basis for action. To this end it develops the outline of the project preparation stage; it gives structure to the work to come. The statement of intent is usually circulated to all specialist sections which are expected to contribute to the project formulation.

This first task is commonly carried out by a 'project manager'. The individual who has been given this responsibility may specialise in project management. This often happens with large companies in the process industries where the continuity of work permits such division of labour. Alternatively, it could be anyone, seconded on a full-time basis or merely charged with an extra duty, who has the responsibility for this specific task. This person may or may not have the status of manager in the wider context of company organisation. The selection and manner of appointment of such a manager is of course a vital part of the preparation planning phase. Much of what will happen as the project develops can be ascribed, for better or for worse, to this particular step. Of course, the selected individual may already have been associated with the previous feasibility analysis.

Next, the project manager, or, if the scale of operation warrants it, his staff, then prepares a timetable for the various stages of project preparation. This includes the definition of the main task constituents. Much of the work here is the coordination of specialist activities, and the timetable has to integrate their respective contributions in a manner which is economic, technologically feasible and consistent with the overall target time. The development of such a programme requires the solution of scheduling and resources problems. For complex situations an elaborate activity network may have to be developed.

In large companies a standard practice for the required organisation and coordination often already exists. Otherwise the framework of coordination has to be developed and this framework has to encompass the different activities of functional analysis and subsequent proposal definition. This is particularly important where the firm is about to embark on a venture which dwarfs what is considered to be the normal project. The accepted organisational assumptions no longer hold when the project is, say, ten times the usual scale.

It is axiomatic that as part of the project organisational development the project manager will be responsible for the definition of the communication system between the project participants, the reporting procedures to top management (where not already defined) and the manner of staff cost control.

Functional analysis

This stage of the preparation process begins when those concerned have received the instructions and guidance they require to carry out their specialist tasks. Not all the specialists can start at once — their entry is determined by the logic of the technology involved. For instance, with a large process plant the electrical engineer can only specify a motor when the mechanical engineer has determined what pump should be used; in turn, the latter waits until the chemical engineer has determined the material flow conditions.

But whatever the timing of their entry, they will be concerned with the analysis of the project brief in the context of their specialisation. They assess the meaning and the feasibility of that brief, the problems it generates and the constraints within which a solution needs to be found. A series of investigations may be called for or outside consultants may need to be retained. A typical illustration is the drilling of test holes for the foundations of a new factory. Without knowledge of the load-bearing soil characteristics it would be impossible to determine the nature or cost of such foundations. The structural stability of the newly-built factory could be affected and thus introduce a special risk. We can thus view the purpose of functional analysis to be the ascertainment of the nature and degree of risk associated with each facet of the project proposal. The investigations and enquiries are designed to eliminate the risks, or at least to reduce them to acceptable proportions. This depends on the ability to control the factors involved. A technical production problem may be fully resolved in a 'controlled' situation; a marketing problem may be hostage to the strategies of others.

Two specific aspects can affect the functional analysis. Firstly, some of the relevant work may have already been carried out at the feasibility analysis stage, i.e. a key problem was anticipated and, in substance, has already been resolved. Secondly, the firm may have established standard practices to which some of the investigations have to conform. For example, a firm may require its design staff to carry out very specific calculations as to the size and costs of process pipelines. In such cases the structure of the investigation is determined by calculation sheets, specification forms and computer packages.

Figure 4.3 lists the more important functional areas of the firm with which analysis will be concerned, namely technology, manufacture, marketing, supplies, personnel. The list is not exclusive; special situations could exist, for instance, where the key aspects of investigation focus on the validity of a patent or the feasibility of a licensing agreement. A straight expansion project might emphasise markets, supplies and human resources as the main subject for investigation. A cost reduction project pays more attention to engineering, plant and process matters.

An important aspect of project management is to spot and to classify all significant problems which the analysis encounters. Some can be contained within their specialist categories; others have wider repercussions. For instance, in the manufacture of antibiotics the problem of bacteriological contamination affects many aspects of process and plant analysis. Again, some problems may be resolved within the specified time by a crash programme of staff concentration. Others, more intractable, may be insoluble within the period of the project preparation horizon. The project intent may have to be restated in order to bypass the problem. Failing that, the project could be in jeopardy. Even the early recognition of this has its merits.

The anticipation, or at least the prompt detection, of problems is part of effective project management; it helps to contain both delay and costs. The onus remains on the project manager to ensure that the magnitude of the problem is matched by corresponding resources. As he is essentially a coordinator — he usually has no line authority over specialist contributors — much will depend on his skills of coordination and communication. (The latter applies both laterally and vertically upwards.)

Functional development

Functional development is a close follower of functional analysis. In practice, the boundary can be quite fuzzy. Analytically speaking, the two can be distinguished as follows: one is concerned with the assessment and resolution of relevant problems, the other is a synthesis of findings. Constituents of the proposal begin to take shape. In the production situation, development means the definition of particular items of plant or, at a more integrated level, the disposition of such plant in a new factory layout. Where technical change is involved it includes the development and design of new plant in the engineering sense. In special cases it can also involve the building and testing of prototype units; we are here at the borderline between development work in the conventional sense and investment preparation. With a marketing or commercial content there could be test marketing and a range of exploratory negotiations.

The investment proposal is not yet defined but some important constituents, around which the proposal mix will be built, are beginning to crystallise. The main criterion at this stage is operational feasibility. Technological feasibility is, of course, a fundamental part of this. Economic feasibility considerations are implied rather than explicit at this stage although an obviously basic cost factor is bound to get attention. However, this is more likely to form part of 'good' design or engineering practice rather than as a component of project evaluation.

With a large technical project content, functional development can be an expensive and time-consuming process. Here the emphasis is on the cost control aspect of project management. Everything is tentative in a financial sense; there is no guarantee that the subsequent capital expenditure submission will be authorised. The problem is the location of the cut-off point. The work should be sufficiently advanced to give confidence in its eventual success, yet without incurring unnecessary losses, should the project have to be stopped.

Proposal definition

This is a more familiar part of the project preparation stage. It is found with every meaningful investment proposal, whereas some of the other modules may not necessarily occur. It takes the different contributions from the development stage and integrates them into one or several propositions. An overall picture emerges. Integration includes here the elimination of inconsistencies or gaps between the specialist contributions.

The defined proposal will be in document form. Its main constituents will be the following:

A statement of objectives. Typically, this could be a statement of output or an increase in production. Alternatively, it might be a statement of product quality or cost reduction. Again, the project objective could be the attainment of a particular step within a broader strategy.

The method of achievement. This is a description as to how the objectives are to be attained. Under this heading would be specified new processes or production methods, i.e. the general outline of the proposed facilities as seen in the context of a given operational situation.

Listing of proposed plant and buildings. This is largely an inventory of the main project constituents. Key plant details which justify operational selection may also be given. Some boards prefer to see the full technical or suppliers' specifications of major plant items. In these cases they usually appear as appendices in the proposal brochure. Similarly, with new buildings or factory sites, architectural schemes and basic layouts are enclosed. In general, the narrative content depends on the complexity of the proposal as well as its organisational environment.

The estimate of capital expenditure. This is a statement of the expected capital cost of the proposal. The total may be expressed as a single value or as a range of figures. With larger projects the overall value is usually broken down into subtotals for key sections within a framework of accounting codes. In a different manner the total may also be expressed in a cash-flow form, showing typically the pattern for equipment deposit and delivery payments. This also applies to progress payments for construction work. Many firms make it a practice to append to the estimate notes as to their accuracy classification and to specify the key assumptions on which the calculations are based. Similarly, contingency requirements are listed, typically, to allow for escalation.

The benefit statement. Where the project is justified on economic grounds the statement will describe the expected net revenue gain due to the proposed capital expenditure. The gain may be due to the extra contribution from sales, either as a result of increased volume or margins. Alternatively, it can be due to cost reduction and, of course, a mixture of the two main sources is also possible. These benefits may be shown for a year, with the implied assumption — not always tenable —

of their continuity; or they are projected over a specified horizon, say, five years. The benefit need not be expressed in quantified economic terms; a safety or welfare argument could be marshalled in its place.

The time scale. A project or, for that matter, any venture without a time scale has no real meaning. The two relevant measures incorporated in the project definition are the duration of the project itself, i.e. the time span during which resources are expended on capital account and the expected life span of the plant in question.

These are the major parts of the proposal and the absence of any one could significantly weaken it. This does not however require complete enumeration every time in a document form. For instance, with routine and relatively minor plant replacement projects some of these statements may be subsumed within established manufacturing policies. But the more important the project, the stronger is the case for an explicit statement in the proposal.

A number of additional features are often found depending on the systems operated by a particular management. Some firms couple the project evaluation with the proposal definition stage. This may reflect organisational philosophy or the commonsense argument that those who prepare the proposal should see for themselves whether it makes economic sense. At the risk of being arbitrary we shall discuss investment evaluation in the next chapter. Before embarking on this, however, there are some observations to be made on the industrial practice of project definition.

Some observations on proposal definition

It is useful to recall the section commencing on page 29 and the large number of capital expenditure applications that need to be processed by any firm of size. Standard presentation helps appraisal and decision, particularly where, as in a portfolio situation, project proposals need to be compared and ranked. Yet such presentation may still conceal differences in interpretation, computation and assumptions, all of which could affect the judgement of the decision makers. This has prompted top management to consider in some detail the whole process of proposal definition. The result is the operating manual or administrative procedure which establishes the principles and detail practice of proposal definition. Proposal definition is usually the substance of the first chapter; subsequent to this come appropriate instructions on the evaluation, presentation and authorisation mechanism of projects.

Three out of four of the associated companies operated such a system. The fourth used five-year forecasts for the planning of expansion in manufacturing capacity. The systems emphasis was on the annual capital expenditure budget for every department and factory rather than on the individual proposal.

All companies had standard capital expenditure application forms. These contained interesting variations in purpose and complexity. The procedure adopted by companies A and B were applicable both to capital expenditure and special revenue expenditure proposals. Companies C and D confined their system to the former. To this purpose their operating instructions defined the term capital expenditure for guidance in project preparation. Company C interpreted it as follows:

'For the purpose of this procedure, Capital Expenditure represents the acquisition of a permanent asset whose value exceeds £50 which has a life of not less than one year and is not usually expended in the normal course of production. It also includes office furniture and equipment whose value exceeds £25... In addition all expenses directly related to the acquisition of these assets shall be included as part of the amounts involved when submitting a request for Capital Expenditure (e.g. installation, freight, duty, rearrangement, dismantling or removal costs)...'

Company D employed the following definition:

'Capital expenditure is defined as:

1.1 Any expenditure that increases, or improves the fixed assets of the business, together with *and* for the purpose *only* of calculating % return:

1.2 Any increase in the net working capital of the business to finance a project. For this purpose net working capital is defined as stock plus debtors less creditors'.

The capital expenditure application was the embodiment of the project proposal. It was essentially a multi-page document. With company A this consisted of a project description, financial summary, details of investment cash needed, cash details of benefit and a cash-flow graph. The company C system incorporated a project summary, cost analysis, machinery and building detail sheets. Company D had a basic capital project form, supported by an evaluation summary, plant list and working capital statement. Apart from these basic documents it had specialist forms for market forecasts, labour cost savings, ingredient savings — to be used by the proposers as required.

The detailed form design reflected each company's manner of project proposal definition. It was rather affected by the prescribed method of project evaluation. It showed what top management regarded as important in a commercial sense, with explicit computation steps for key data. Periodic updating of the forms allowed for systems changes and the effect of government measures relating to investments.

All forms required a statement of justification for the proposed scheme. The justification could be a specific and newly-established expectation or a reference to an already agreed and documented decision. In some cases the proposer had to select a justification category, e.g. in company B he had to choose from the following defined and illustrated classification:

'Company Reorganisation

Diversification into New Products
Expansion of Capacity for Existing Lines
Others
Profit Improvement Projects
Quality, Hygiene, Welfare and Amenity
Replacements
Safety, Security and Statutory Requirements.'

The relationship between a particular proposal and the general capital expenditure budget seemed to get only a partial acknowledgment in the documents. Only companies C and D required the proposer to refer to a budget allocation, if any. This does, however, suggest an interesting two-stage mechanism. The first stage is the inclusion, without promise, of a particular proposal in the capital expenditure budget. (We are referring here to the type of project which can normally be financed by the company's depreciation cash-flow.) The second stage is the actual evaluation in the conventional sense, which determines the fate of the proposal. The first stage indicates a periodic 'draft' dialogue between project proposers (or sponsors at departmental management level) and the investment decision makers.

The administrative instructions gave considerable attention to the 'form-filling' parts of the proposal. Guidance and illustrations were commonly given to ensure that the forms would be used consistently and universally. This included, for instance, instructions on graph preparation by company A. Company D used flow diagrams to explain to users some of the key aspects of preparation and work coordination. Other interesting features of instructions were requirements as to the discussion of risks, an account of feasible alternatives, considered but not submitted, and comparisons with competitors.

The manner of yield calculation was made very explicit by company A to ensure that all staff concerned understood its particular pattern. This reflected its policy that those who prepared a proposal should be the first to evaluate it. However, it did not specify a set rate of return. Only company C gave such instructions: its staff had to assess projects on a 15% DCF present-value basis.

The urgency level of some projects was recognised by company C. It had a procedure for 'emergency requests' in the case of fire, damage caused by the elements, unexpected breakdowns in production, etc. The personnel concerned had to decide whether to use the standard procedure or to seek verbal approval which was confirmed by an emergency release form. This is an interesting reminder of operational conditions in a capital-intensive process industry.

All systems had definite rules as to who was responsible for form completion. Provisions were made on the capital request summary form for the signatures of the originators, verifying specialists and appropriate operational managers. Company D had an explicit responsibility chart for this. A simplified version of this is shown in Figure 4.4.

Check list: Project preparation

Basic

1. Does our company have a standard practice and forms for the preparation and submission of capital expenditure projects?
2. Who is responsible for the maintenance and updating of specified procedures?
3. When were they last reviewed? Does each form have a date and a revision number?
4. Who should have a copy of the procedures?
5. Are the procedures well integrated with other standard practices? Any gaps or overlaps?

Feasibility

1. What happens to good project ideas in our company?

CAPITAL PROJECT FORM	Originator	Evaluating Accountant	Factory Director	Divisional Controller	Group Finance	Group Production Services Director
Project number				x	x	
Location	x					
Description of project	x					
Estimated commissioning date	x					
Estimated life of asset	x					
Asset classification	x					
Cost figures	x					
Working capital		x				
Budget details	x					
Justification category	x					
Additional justification	x					
Predicted performance		x				
Signatures — Originator — Reviewing function — Evaluating Accountant — Reviewing Accountant	x	x	x	x		x
Approved/rejected		x	x	x	x	
Appendices Evaluating summary		x				
Summary (main points)		x				
Analysis and detail of gross cost	x					

Responsibility for completion ———→

Figure 4.4 Example of project verification responsibility chart

2. Think of a good project idea which was not developed. Why did it not survive?
3. What is our catchment system for ideas?
4. What techniques do you use for generating ideas? Brainstorming? Lateral thinking? Value analysis?
5. Do we have a suggestion scheme? Can its contribution be increased?
6. Are there simple guidelines for feasibility analysis?
7. Design a simple form for idea feasibility assessment.
8. How would you retrieve such an idea in two years' time?

Plant definition

1. What are the operational requirements?
   a. Volume/rate of output.
   b. Quality.
   c. Equipment Reliability.
   d. Safety.
   e. Operating Costs.
   f. Manning.
   g. Efficiencies.
2. Who will be affected by these requirements? Have they been told verbally, in writing?
3. What are the implications of these requirements on:
   a. Other plant.
   b. Buildings.
   c. Services (including effluents).
   d. Storage facilities.
   e. Material handling.
   f. Roads, access, gangways?
4. What will be the effects on industrial relations?
   a. Changes in techniques.
   b. Staff transfers.
   c. Redundancies.
   d. New skills, re-grading.
   e. Recruitment, training.

Purchased equipment

1. Have you satisfied yourself as to the supplier's capacity and reputation? (Vendor analysis)
2. Does the proposed equipment meet your requirements? If it falls short in some respects, what will be the operational implications and costs?
3. Is the offered equipment
   a. Really proven?
   b. About to become obsolescent?
4. Does the quoted price cover such costs as:
   a. Transport.
   b. Custom duties.
   c. Insurances.
   d. Installation and other site costs.
   e. Commissioning.
   f. Operator training.
   g. Packaging.
   h. Key spares?
5. How reliable is delivery? What would be the costs to you of a delay of 1, 3, 6 months?
6. What would be the life-cycle costs?
   a. Operational: labour, material, services.
   b. Maintenance: labour, material, spare inventory costs.
   c. Downtimes due to breakdowns or malfunction.
7. What backup can you expect from the supplier?
   a. Guarantees.
   b. Service.
   c. Instruction manuals.
   d. Parts lists, spares.
   e. Special tools and test equipment.

Newly-developed plant

1. Have you the design, engineering and manufacturing resources?
2. How are staff resources costed and budgeted?
3. Have your staff sufficient relevant experience?

4. Has a prototype unit been developed? By you? By others?
5. Has the prototype plant been adequately tested on production runs?
6. If you are scaling up from a model or a pilot plant, what problems can be expected at full scale?
7. What will be the development costs from the prototype stage? Right from the beginning?
8. Many development projects overrun their budget. What would be the consequences if development costs were 50%, 100%, 200% higher?
9. Could the development work be contracted out? At what cost?
10. How long will the development project take?
11. Are there side benefits with the developed plant, such as equipment sales to third parties?
12. Will you need specialist suppliers for parts and subsystems?
13. Could there be patent complications?

Proposal definition

1. Has the plant been fully specified and listed?
2. Is there a proper statement of the basis of design or operating principles for the new equipment?
3. Are key plant and layout drawings available?
4. What assumptions need to be listed about inputs, efficiencies and output levels?
5. What will be the expected plant life?
6. Will any existing plant be replaced? How will it be disposed of? Will there be residual cash flows?
7. How long will the project take to implement if authorised?
8. Have you obtained the full capital cost of equipment installed and connected up?
9. Have you included the provision of plant services (if any), site and building work?
10. Will there be royalty or know-how payments?

11. Are there any special revenue costs to be allowed for?
12. What project management and engineering charges have to be included?
13. Is working capital needed?

Reference

1. Beattie, C.J. and Reader, R.D., *Quantitative Management in R & D.* Chapman and Hall (London, 1971)

5 Project evaluation

The basic project preparation task leads to a defined project proposal. Two of the most important constituents of the proposal development task are the computation of capital expenditure and the expected project benefits. The job of project evaluation is to relate these two estimates, i.e. to establish the worth of the project in financial terms. Most of the chapter will be devoted to this form of evaluation but before doing so let us see project evaluation in perspective.

As evaluation only has meaning when there is something tangible to consider, a proposal must be formulated first. Evaluation need not, however, wait until the preparation task is complete particularly where preparation costs are considerable. Two of the main decision stages of the preparation process include a form of evaluation, however tentative that might be. One can see evaluation at several levels, each with organisational and systems implications:

The strategic and policy level. This assesses the relevance of the investment proposal in relation to company objectives and policies. Such evaluation may be carried out by a board committee or in large corporations by a corporate planning department. Plant investment projects at this level may be concerned with major extensions, the building of new factories or basic changes in production processes. The evaluation would obviously take place at an early stage of project formulation.

The implementation evaluation level. This level presumes the proposal relevance but examines every aspect of intent. It is concerned with operating statements, financial commitments and expectations, forecasts and all claims made by the project preparation group or sponsoring management. The biggest opportunity here is to question the assumptions on which the case for an investment rests. Project alternatives may be proposed and considered with the purpose of optimising the worth of a proposition. Risk analysis and financial evaluation techniques may also be applied. This level of evaluation is applicable to all plant projects of substance where there is an element of novelty or uncertainty. Much of such an evaluation may be carried out explicitly or intuitively by a senior line manager, with or without the help of a personal assistant or someone specially seconded for such purpose. In large companies this form of evaluation is often the responsibility of a management services group.

The financial evaluation level. This level accepts the soundness of the operating and technical premises of the proposition for which others take the responsibility. It is confined to the direct assessment of the project financial data, particularly the claimed benefits, or, alternatively, verifies the financial statements prepared by the project preparation group or project sponsors. This evaluation is usually carried out by the accounting function, or, where the scale, importance or the politics of the project warrant it, by consulting accountants. Typically, the company auditors may be retained for such a purpose.

The classification of different evaluation levels is a helpful concept although in practice one can expect some overlap. The distinction between the project preparers and evaluators may be reinforced by the organisational framework, for instance where the preparers are at factory level and the evaluators are attached to head office. But in the absence of such framework, particularly with the medium to small firm, this distinction may be blurred. Even on the time scale of preparation and evaluation there may be some overlap. Where a complex project requires extensive preparation work, some evaluation tasks may begin on completed sections, before the whole project is finalised in detail.

With our concentration on financial evaluation it is helpful to remember that projects with non-economic objectives or nonquantifiable benefits are not amenable to this form of analysis — although some forms of cost-benefit assessment might be applied. Typically, two forms of project benefit cannot be properly judged on financial criteria: (i) *Social welfare benefits.* For example, a company may undertake substantial capital expenditures on a new works canteen, employee amenities or to bring the factory in line with the requirements of the Health and Safety at Work Act 1974. (ii) *Functional benefits.* The benefits can be perceived but are difficult to measure. Thus an investment can result in a better company reputation, more customer goodwill, etc. Its precise impact on the company's financial performance is, however, hard to define.

The background to evaluation

This section will consider some of the background factors which influence the financial evaluation of a project. Whilst some of these factors might not become explicit it is seldom that an evaluation is carried out in a 'vacuum'.

Capital expenditure forecasts

These are usually long term by nature, typically for a period of 2-5 years. The extent to which companies make long-term forecasts of capital expenditure is, generally speaking, a function of their overall long-term planning activity. The systematic development of such forecasts was most noticeable with company B. Within the framework of its five-year sales forecast it was standard practice to prepare a three-year forecast of new capital expenditure, together with an approximate cash outflow profile. Such forecasts at group level were built up from individual factory requirements.

Again, the intent of company C was explicit. Its policy statement on the control of capital expenditure indicated: 'It is a future objective that Managers will also estimate major items required for the four years following the above budget year under review. This section will be implemented when the overall Company long-term plan has been developed.'

Annual capital expenditure budgets

These are, of course, an integral part of the basic system of budgetary control and thus subject to the general discipline of specified and timetabled submission, modification and approval. Capital expenditure intentions are thus evaluated and integrated within the company's trading prospect and overall cash flow. The capital expenditure budget is normally divided into land and buildings, plant and machinery and other categories.

Understandably, the amount budgeted for capital expenditure each year is affected by a number of considerations. First and foremost is the company's trading position and its general financial state, particularly its liquidity and ability to obtain the required capital at the prevailing rates of interest. Secondly, the annual budget may express the implementation of long-term plans. From an operational point of view the company will also be guided by past experience; for instance, it may set aside a certain part of its depreciation cash flow for replacement and modernisation. Apart from these general considerations a number of prepared and evaluated projects may wait, provisionally approved, for inclusion in the next budget.

The actual administration of the capital expenditure budget can vary considerably. Where we have the specific and evaluated project the budget inclusion is tantamount to authorisation. But much of the budget can remain a general provision for which a particular claim has to be made without any prior guarantee of authorisation. The budget expresses, in essence, the constraint of the capital rationing situation. This applies particularly to minor expenditures within the discretion of line management.

It is not, however, necessary for every project to be earmarked or provided for by a budget. But then it has to be sufficiently attractive or necessary to be considered as an extra-budget claim.

Plant depreciation policies

A company's depreciation policy is, of course, a significant parameter in its investment evaluation. Its view on the depreciation rate to be adopted determines plant life in accounting terms. The end of such life terminates the stream of benefits which the calculation can take into account. The physical and operating characteristics of the plant after its notional demise in terms of book value is a separate matter. The DCF calculation is thus affected by a time scale cut-off point, while the return on capital computation is in any case affected by the specific provision for depreciation from the gross benefit.

Government fiscal measures

It is common knowledge that government actions affect project decisions. They can also influence the pattern of project evaluation. They affect projects either by providing an incentive, such as regional investment grants, or as a discouragement, such as an increase in corporation tax. One can also distinguish between direct and indirect effects.

The rate of taxation on the generated benefit is of course a key factor in the evaluation of the net project yield and the corresponding cash flow. Similarly, tax allowances can have a major effect on computations. Project evaluation can be on a 'gross' or 'net of tax' basis. There is a strong case for the 'net' approach, particularly where the project sponsor or preparation group has to make the first evaluation. Taxation, it is argued, is a regrettable fact of life and an appraisal which ignores it is unrealistic. Nevertheless, some companies prefer to view propositions 'gross' rather than 'net'. A company's tax liability is hostage to many other considerations. Many capital projects are for modest or relatively small amounts, taxable profits are uncertain and there is much to be gained from a simple, consistent system freed from the variability of government fiscal measures. Taxation can be allowed for globally by specifying higher cut-off rates. The occasional large, strategic project warrants special treatment anyway, but the other, say, 98% of projects would gain from simplification.

A related policy aspect, which is considerably affected by fiscal measures, is the treatment of certain research and development expenditures. If these are capitalised they can have a significant influence on project values and returns.

The data for evaluation

Investment appraisal relates the prospective capital expenditure to the future cash flow it generates. It follows from this that most of the data to be fed into the appraisal task concern these two categories. They are a function of the proposal itself. The unit of account is money, expressed against a time scale. Apart from this there is a special type of information which, for the want of a better term, we can call the parameters of calculation. These reflect the standard practice of the company, e.g. the depreciation or the discount rates to be used.

The required capital expenditure

This statement is usually divided into two categories: the expenditure on fixed assets and the required additional working capital. In the context of investment in production plant the fixed assets normally account for the greater part of the expenditure. However, it need not be so. For instance, a new product may only need one or two extra machines, while the remainder of its production route uses existing equipment. The greater part of the investment may then be to finance the expected sales volume. It is also possible for either category to have a negative value, i.e. to give rise to some dis-investment. This can be quite common where new equipment improves a production process and permits the reduction of work in progress or inventories. Again, it is possible to have an investment project involving a reduction in fixed assets, but except for certain lease-back operations, these are very infrequent and may be ignored here.

Considering first the expenditure on fixed assets, the state-ment represents a definitive estimate for the purpose of authorisation. Depending on the nature of the work or the type of plant involved it may be accurate to within ±5-10%. The following are the main categories of expense for major projects. For more modest schemes only some of the cate-gories will apply. Each category is also capable of further subdivision.

Expenditure on fixed assets
1. Site acquisition costs.
2. Acquisition expenses.
3. Site clearance and preparation.
4. Buildings. Erection and alterations.
5. Plant and building services.
6. Plant foundations.
7. Machinery and process plant. This includes associated costs, such as freight, insurance or duty.
8. Plant process and services connections.
9. Installation and erection costs.
10. Tools and fixtures.
11. Personnel, welfare and administrative facilities.
12. Capitalised research and expenditure costs.
13. Design costs.

14. Project management costs.
15. Professional fees.
16. General site costs.
17. Know-how or lump-sum licence payments.

From the overall total fixed assets costs the disposal proceeds of existing redundant plant are deducted. If such disposal proceeds have a time lag these can be discounted to the period of receipt.

Changes in working capital
1. Inventory levels.
2. Work-in-progress values.
3. Debtors.
4. Creditors.

The estimated salvage value of the project assets at the end of the plant life are treated as a specific receipt accruing in the year of disposal. However, where extended plant life is presumed and the proceeds are likely to be small and uncertain, such salvage values may be neglected. Again, the partial or complete recovery of working capital at the end of operations is treated as a receipt at that time.

The definition of project benefits

In this context we are concerned with investment in production plant which is justified on economic grounds. Other, less tangible benefits may also emerge, but these are disregarded for our purpose. Where, then, are the likely sources of these benefits?

In our analysis we are only concerned with identifiable, incremental changes in costs and incomes; i.e. the net effect the project has on the company's cash flow. 'Notional' cash flows and overhead apportionment assumptions are irrelevant to the analysis. The project benefits may be derived from operating financial data under two broad headings:

Changes in revenue. Typically these could be due to:
1. An increase in the net effective sales volume, assuming

constant prices. The net contribution from the extra sales would constitute the change in cash flow.

2. Higher sales receipts without major changes in volume. Examples of this are premium quality payments, or the reduction in 'seconds'.
3. Any mixture of (1) and (2).
4. Patent, royalty or licensing income.

Changes in costs. Many categories of operating costs could be affected by a project. The following are the most important:

1. Direct labour costs of production, including terminal costs for redundancies, etc.
2. Indirect labour and staff costs.
3. Overtime payments (non-productive overtime cost element).
4. Maintenance charges.
5. Plant services: power, gas, air, etc.
6. Tooling, where treated as a revenue charge.
7. Materials. Direct production materials and indirect materials, such as catalysts, refrigerants, lubricants, etc.
8. Consumables.
9. Scrap and rectification charges.
10. Insurances, rates, rent.
11. Transport costs.
12. Stock carrying charges.
13. Finance charges, e.g. in respect of working capital, such as work in progress, debtors.
14. Sub-contracting charges.

In many instances the evaluation involves the balancing of savings under some headings against additional costs in other categories. The resultant net figure constitutes the gross project benefit. It is axiomatic that the relevant cost data should be of sufficient accuracy so as not to vitiate the meaning of the investment evaluation which makes use of it. There is little point in evaluation refinement when the source data is rough.

The basic appraisal techniques

There are moments when the brilliant (or lucky) manager can perceive in a flash the worth of a proposition and without calculation proceeds with the correct action. Lesser mortals have to do their homework. For this purpose some well-established appraisal techniques are available. There is a family name for each major type; within it, are a number of variants. The main techniques are as follows:

(a) The payback method.
(b) The return on investment analysis.
(c) The discounted cash flow technique (DCF).

Before considering the details and respective merits of these techniques it would be helpful if we made explicit some of the principles underlying investment appraisal.

The first principle is the *recovery of the investment*. Whatever the initial yield, the ultimate realisation of the investment is essential. The project must at least generate its own depreciation cash flow. The second is one of *adequacy of yield,* considering a firm's total business situation. This subsumes such aspects as the cost of finance to the firm and the risks it is willing to take. The third is the *time value of money*. This principle has not had full attention in the past but with high interest and inflation rates it cannot be disregarded. Only the DCF method incorporates this third principle.

The payback method

The concept of this method is simple: it measures the time which elapses after the initial capital outlay until the cash flow of generated benefits equals the original investment. Graphically it can be shown as in Figure 5.1.

The general case is as follows:

If E = the project capital expenditure and R_i = the project benefit in the 'i'th period, then the payback period is determined by the value of t which solves the equation

$$E = \sum_{i=0}^{i=t} R_i$$

The symbol $\sum$ is the Greek capital letter called sigma. It means here 'the sum of'. In our case it denotes the sum of all the benefits from the moment we start — zero time — until the 't'the period.

The economic acceptability of a project is then dependent on whether this established value of t is more or less than a prescribed time period T.

Consider a simple example:

Capital cost of new machine	£10000
Resultant annual savings	5000

In cash flow terms this means that the outlay will be recovered over two years — the payback period. Assuming now that the company operates at a profit and we have, say:

Corporation tax	50%
First year allowance	100%

The cash outflow due to the investment is taken to be instantaneous, it occurs in year 0. The cash inflow for year one will have two constituents. First there will be a tax saving of £5000 because the whole of the investment can be deducted from taxable profit. The second part will be the generated benefit of £5000 on which the company will have to pay corporation tax at 50% reducing that cash flow constituent to £2500. Again, after two years the outstanding balance will be cleared, this time by a composition of tax saving and taxed benefits. If the tax on generated benefits is paid in the following tax year the cash recovery is already after twelve months provided the lagged tax payment is covered by savings in year two.

If the specified recovery period for a project is two years then obviously this proposition will be acceptable.

Figure 5.1 Cash flow over the payback period

We have a simple, but rather crude, method here. No allowance is made for the timing of proceeds, nor is any note taken of the cash flow after the payback period. The method is inadequate for systematic comparison and rigorous analysis. Its conceptual simplicity is not an advantage if it discourages a more thorough enquiry; its usefulness is more at the initial feasibility appraisal. It is sometimes also used as a short-cut check for minor operational proposals. In such cases there may already be strong technological arguments and the economic case seems so overwhelming that no refined calculation is needed.

There is a valuable aspect to the payback graph shown in Figure 5.1. The total area below the zero line is a function of time and money. Multiplying this area by an interest rate will give the financial cost of the committed money. Thus, if the average amount outstanding were, say, £10000 and the payback period five years, then the interest cost over the payback period at 10% would be 10000 × 5 × 0.1 = £5000. This type of evaluation can be salutary to engineers and managers responsible for the detailed dispositions of a plant project. Other things equal, the ordering, installation, commissioning and running of production plant should minimise the below the line area.

The return on investment analysis

The horizon is now the expected plant life, not the payback period which may be only a modest fraction of the former. The return on investment method measures in percentage terms the benefit for period 'i' against the original investment. In general, we take the rate of return for year 'i' to be r_i

$$\text{where} \quad r_i = \frac{R_i}{E} \cdot 100\%$$

Taking our previous example and using the simplest form of measurement, the return on capital will be

$$\frac{\text{Annual Saving}}{\text{Investment}} \times 100\% = \frac{5000 \times 100\%}{10\,000} = 50\%$$

Where the returns vary over the life of the plant 'T' we obtain an average rate of return r_a where

$$r_a = \frac{100}{T} \left(\sum_{i=0}^{i=T} r_i \right) \% = \frac{100}{T} \left(\sum_{i=0}^{i=T} \frac{R_i}{E} \right) \%$$

For instance, if our machine had a working life of four years and its returns for years one, two, three and four were 40%, 50%, 60% and 70% respectively, the average rate of return would come to 55%. The rate of return can be measured gross or net of depreciation. If there were no allowance for depreciation this would presume an infinite machine life. Such an assumption would, of course, be untenable. As we shall see in Chapter 7, when we come to plant replacement, the economic life of a machine is not only affected by its deterioration in use but also by competitive technical developments. It is not very easy to make a precise forecast of machine life. A conservative estimate tends to keep it on the short side; a thin proposition may survive with an extended life span. It is important here that a company establishes a standard life forecast practice based on equipment categories of which it has had adequate experience.

Take, for instance, two alternative life spans for our machine: first two years, then five years. Further, assume straight-line depreciation and no equipment salvage value at the end of its working life. On that basis, with a two-year life, the provision for depreciation would have to be £5000 per annum to recover the investment. As a result the generated annual savings of £5000 would reduce to zero after depreciation, i.e. there is no return on the investment. For a five-year period we need to put aside £2000 per annum, leaving an after-depreciation benefit of £3000 per annum. This corresponds to a 30% return on the initial investment. A change in the expected equipment life forecast can thus be a major influence on project attractiveness.

So far, rates of return have been related to the initial investment. However, the accumulation of depreciation funds means the recovery of the investment with time. The after-depreciation project benefits could then more usefully be related to the outstanding sum. If the benefits remain constant this will have a gratifying effect on the rates of return. Another alternative would be to use the mean asset book value for the whole of the equipment life. Consider again our machine with a five-year life. (See Table 5.1.) If a mean book value of £6000 were taken, then the rate of return over the five years would be 50%. Year six shows the situation if the equipment survives its book life and continues to make the same savings. From an accounting point of view there is a strong temptation to keep the plant going for ever!

Table 5.1

Year	1	2	3	4	5	6
Saving (£)	5000	5000	5000	5000	5000	5000
Depreciation (£)	2000	2000	2000	2000	2000	0
Book value of machine (£)	10000	8000	6000	4000	2000	0
Benefit after Depreciation (£)	3000	3000	3000	3000	3000	5000
Return on book value (%)	30	37.5	50	75	150	Infinity

Again, the computation can be further refined in the context of profitable operations by allowing for the appropriate rate of corporation tax and initial allowance.

Generally speaking, the basic method has the advantage of easy comparison with the returns of financial investment. It can be readily related to the yield of quoted company shares or the interest rate on borrowed money. There is still no provision, however, for the time element of money. Despite such a limitation this form of analysis is widely used.

The discounted cash flow (DCF) technique

The concept of discounted cash flow has long been associated with banking and insurance calculations, whenever the passage of time and the use of money over such periods was involved. In essence, the concept is concerned with the flow of money in terms of amounts and timing. It allows, in the form of compound interest, for the time-lag between the actual disbursements and the consequent receipts. It permits, with the use of present value tables, the collation of all cash flows irrespective of direction and incidence. In this manner a valid comparison between *capital* expenditure now and subsequent *revenue* benefits can be established.

There are a number of different applications of the basic DCF technique, but before describing these in detail it would help to introduce the concept of present value. Imagine you had a deposit of £100 with a bank or building society and that you obtained an interest payment of 10% at the end of each year of deposit. As a result the sum of principal and interest would amount to £110 at the end of year one and it would further compound to £121 at the end of year two, etc. The general case can be expressed by the formula:

$$X = A (1 + r)^n$$

where X = amount accumulated

A = principal sum to start with

r = rate of interest

n = number of years of accumulation

Taking our particular illustration for year two we have

$$£121 = 100 (1 + 0.10)^2$$

This, in substance, is the effect of compounding which makes a given sum today worth more at some future date. Discounting is the opposite process; it takes a given sum at a future date and expresses it at today's value. Thus, the sum of £121 in two years' time is worth less at this moment. Taking

the same interest rate and time span of our previous example
we come back to our original deposit of £100. Instead of
multiplying by $(1 + 0.10)^2$ we divide by this amount. The
general relationship is given by

$$Y = \frac{B}{(1 + r)^n}$$

where B = a cash flow in year 'n'

Y = the present value of that cash flow, given a rate
of interest 'r'

for all positive values of 'n', i.e. the future, the expression

$$\frac{1}{(1 + r)^n}$$

is less than one. This expression is known as the discount
factor. In our illustration, when r = 0.10 and n = 2, its value
is 0.826. It will be noted that the higher the rate of interest,
also known as the rate of discount, the lower will be the discount factors. Again, as 'n' increases the factor values
diminish further. Discount factors are normally tabulated as
shown in Appendix B.

The yield or rate of return method

The purpose of this method is to find a rate of return for the
discounting of future receipts after a given project outlay has
been made. The project disbursement needs to be recovered.
Normally, this will be done over a number of periods, with
each revenue benefit making a contribution to the recovery of
the outlay and servicing the interest on the outstanding
amount. The greater the revenue benefits, the higher will be
the interest rate at which the outstanding capital sum can be
serviced. Eventually there comes a stage when all the revenue
cash flows are used to repay the investment and to meet the
interest charges. It is for that point of balance that we have to
find the interest rate.

It should be remembered that the recovery of the investment is already included in the calculation. Therefore, no provision needs to be made for depreciation; we are simply concerned with cash flows. The subsequent disposition of these cash flows in the financial accounting context is quite a separate matter.

The general principle of the method can be shown as follows:

let E = the project capital expenditure

R_i = the project benefit in the 'i'th period
(i = 1, 2, ...T) measured at end of period

T = the expected project or equipment life

r = the rate of return to be established.

Allowing for the passage of time, the present value at time 0 of the future receipts will be as follows:

for $\quad R_1 \quad$ it will be $\quad \dfrac{R_1}{1 + r}$

$\qquad R_2 \quad$ it will be $\quad \dfrac{R_2}{(1 + r)^2}$

$\cdots\cdots\cdots\cdots\cdots\cdots$

$\qquad R_1 \quad$ it will be $\quad \dfrac{R_i}{(1 + r)^i} \qquad$ etc.

The total present value (or discounted value) of these benefits will be:

$$\frac{R_1}{(1 + r)} + \frac{R_2}{(1 + r)^2} + \cdots \frac{R_i}{(1 + r)^i} + \cdots \frac{R_T}{(1 + r)^T}$$

$$= \sum_{i = 1}^{i = T} \frac{R_i}{(1 + r)^i}$$

For total outlay recovery this value needs to be equal to the initial investment, thus

$$\sum_{i=1}^{i=T} \frac{R_i}{(1 + r)^i} = E$$

Alternatively this expression can be put in the following form:

$$\sum_{i=1}^{i=T} \frac{R_i}{(1 + r)^i} - E = 0$$

The value of 'r' is the unknown in the equation and our task is to find it. When we have found the value of 'r' which solves this equation we have found the interest rate at which the project has zero net present value (NPV), i.e. our immediate outlay is balanced by the future discounted receipts at that rate of interest. For all other interest rates there will not be this balance and we shall have a NPV with a value other than zero. If a particular rate is pitched too low the NPV will be positive; if our rate is too high the NPV will be negative. This property is very useful in calculating the rate of return, as we shall see in subsequent examples.

Example 1
Consider, initially, a new production plant with a capital cost of £100000, an expected working life of five years and yielding the following net cash flow (see Table 5.2).

How can we best calculate our rate of return? The first thing we note is that the net project receipts come to £150000 over the five years. We recover our investment outlay and £50000 is available for interest payments. To make a first assessment of the rate of return we calculate the project NPVs at key rates, say at 10%, 20% and 30%. Using the discount tables in Appendix B we obtain the results shown in Table 5.3. The respective NPVs are plotted on graph paper and a net present value curve is obtained as per Figure 5.2. If the curve is laid

Table 5.2

Year	1	2	3	4	5
Cash flow (£)	40000	30000	30000	25000	25000

Table 5.3

Year	Net cash Flow £	At 10%		At 20%		At 30%	
		Discount factor	Present value	Discount factor	Present value	Discount factor	Present value
0	(100000)	1.000	(100000)	1.000	(100000)	1.000	(100000)
1	40000	0.909	36360	0.833	33320	0.769	30760
2	30000	0.826	24780	0.694	20820	0.592	17760
3	30000	0.751	22530	0.579	17370	0.455	13650
4	25000	0.683	17075	0.482	12050	0.350	8750
5	25000	0.621	15525	0.402	10050	0.269	6725
Total net present value (£)			16270		(6390)		(22355)

(figures in brackets are negative)

out on a sheet of graph paper it will be noted that it will cut the zero NPV line between 16% and 17%. To come nearer to the actual rate of return the project NPVs are calculated for these rates. (See Table 5.4). We can now calculate the more precise rate as

$$16 + \frac{1700}{1700 + 400} = 16.8\%$$

Although greater accuracy is possible one should remember the approximate nature of the input data. For practical purposes the calculation need not go beyond one decimal point. The more precise discount rate can also be obtained by graphical interpolation from the two NPV figures.

Table 5.4

Year	Net cash Flow (£)	At 16% Discount factor	At 16% Present value	At 17% Discount factor	At 17% Present value
0	(100000)	1.000	(100000)	1.000	(100000)
1	40000	0.862	34480	0.855	34200
2	30000	0.743	22290	0.731	21930
3	30000	0.641	19230	0.624	18720
4	25000	0.552	13800	0.534	13350
5	25000	0.476	11900	0.456	11400
Total net present value (£)			1700		(400)

Having found the rate of return for our project example we can now analyse the cash flow pattern. The cash flow for each year is divided into interest and repayment and the right column shows how the outstanding capital sum is reduced over time. The outstanding amount at the end of one year earns 16.8% interest in the next year. (See Table 5.5.) Example 1 was a relatively simple illustration of the rate of return method. If we now bring in taxation aspects we can see their discounting implications.

Example 2
For the same project assume now corporation tax at 50%, an initial plant allowance of 100% and an equipment salvage value of £5000 at the end of its working life. Tax allowances and payments normally accrue one year after the cash flow. The project computation would then look as per Table 5.6:

The relatively high rate of project return is largely the effect of the initial allowance which, by its tax saving, permits the early repayment of a substantial part of the capital expenditure. The later cash flows look correspondingly better when related to the outstanding capital sums despite the effect of corporation tax. The payment of this tax a year after

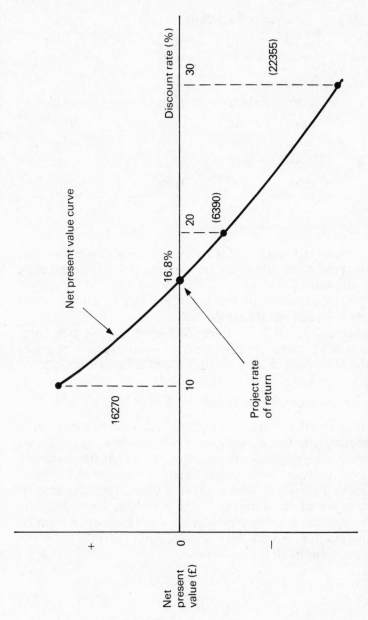

Figure 5.2 Derivation of net present value curve

Table 5.5 Analysis of cash flow pattern

End of Year	Net cash flow (£)	Interest at 16.8%	Capital repayment	Capital outstanding
0	(100000)	—	—	100000
1	40000	16800	23200	76800
2	30000	12901	17099	59701
3	30000	10029	19971	39730
4	25000	6674	18326	21404
5	25000	3596	21404	0
Total		50000	100000	

the appropriate receipt is, of course, an important advantage. Should the initial allowance be less then 100% the remaining tax allowances will have to be spread over the years of accrual. The effect of the balancing charge on the plant disposal receipt should also be noted.

Example 2 can be further developed to suit particular company situations. Further cash flows, irrespective of origin or direction can readily be incorporated in the calculation.

The net present value method

In this alternative approach the evaluation is based on a previously specified annual rate of return — say, s%. This rate is usually based on a minimum return which the company expects to obtain from an investment before it even begins to consider it. Such a return takes into account the rate of interest which the company has to pay to attract finance, its own degree of optimism/pessimism about business prospects, a margin for project management etc. On this basis the present value of all future benefits will be

$$\sum_{i=1}^{i=T} \frac{R_i}{(1+s)^i}$$

Table 5.6   Example 2 — After tax project rate of return

Year	Capital investment	Tax saving on investment	Project income	Tax paid on project income	Net cash flow	At 17%		At 18%	
						Discount factor	Present value	Discount factor	Present value
0	(100000)				(100000)	1.000	(100000)	1.000	(100000)
1		50000	40000		90000	0.855	76950	0.848	76320
2			30000	(20000)	10000	0.731	7310	0.718	7180
3			30000	(15000)	15000	0.629	9360	0.718	9135
4			25000	(15000)	10000	0.534	5340	0.516	5160
5	5000		25000	(12500)	17500	0.456	7980	0.437	7647
6		(2500)	—	(12500)	(15000)	0.390	(5850)	0.370	(5550)
Total	(95000)	47500	150000	75000	27500		1090		(108)

DCF Rate of return $= 17 + \dfrac{1090}{1090 + 108} = 17.9\%$

and the net present value (NPV) will be

$$\sum_{i=1}^{i=T} \frac{R_i}{(1 + s)^i} - E$$

The higher this value the more profitable will be the investment. If the value is negative this means that the rate of return is less than the required rate set by the company. If the value is zero the project return equals the specified rate. The set rate of s%, of course, requires most careful consideration. The net present value technique is simple and quick in application. It has the advantage of ready comparison between a number of competitive projects, particularly if a situation of 'capital rationing' applies.

As an illustration of this method, let us assume a company specified a discount rate of 15% after tax. Taking the after tax cash flow of Example 2, the tabulation would look like Table 5.7.

Table 5.7

Year	Net cash Flow (£)	At 15% Discount factor	At 15% Present value
0	(100000)	1.000	(100000)
1	90000	0.870	78300
2	10000	0.756	7560
3	15000	0.658	9870
4	10000	0.572	5720
5	17500	0.497	8698
6	(15000)	0.432	(6480)
Total NPV			£3668

The project NPV, at the specified company discount rate of 15%, amounts to £3668.

The profitability index

Where plant projects queue for authorisation, but funds are insufficient for the total portfolio, then priority ranking becomes important. This ordering could be done on a rate of return or the NPV basis. A company may have a number of project proposals which meet the specified (or minimum) rate of return; some can be accepted, others have to be left. (Although prevalent, one hopes that this is only a short run position and that in the longer term the company can make suitable funding arrangements to take all its project opportunities.) Anyway, as funds are rationed the amounts requested become particularly important. Project scale needs to be related to project worth. However, the NPV method does not discriminate adequately between projects which vary substantially in size. For instance, project A may cost twice as much as project B but its NPV is 50% higher. Superficially, it looks more attractive but its DCF return rate is, in fact, lower. This seeming dilemma can be overcome by the concept of the profitability index, PI. Using the previous notation, this can be defined by the expression

$$PI = \frac{\text{Present value of future benefits}}{\text{Project capital expenditure}} =$$

$$\frac{1}{E} \left[\sum_{i=1}^{i=T} \frac{R_i}{(1+s)^i} \right]$$

Taking our example with the specified discount rate of 15%, our profitability index would be $103\,668/100\,000 = 1.03668$. Alternatively, one can use the net present value contribution (NPVC) per £ of invested funds. We would then have

$$NPVC = \frac{\text{Project NPV}}{\text{Project capital expenditure}} =$$

$$\frac{1}{E} \left[\sum_{i=1}^{i=T} \frac{R_i}{(1+s)^i} - E \right] = PI - 1$$

The NPVC for our previous example will be 0.036 68, i.e. every £ invested would not only earn the required interest at 15% but would also produce an equivalent gain of 3.668 pence.

Bromwich[1], in his study of capital budgeting, illustrates the use of profitability indices in the fund rationing situation.

Applying the DCF technique

Discounted cash flow is not only a convenient tool for plant investment appraisal; it can also be applied to many related problems, particularly in the project preparation stage. There are also variants of the technique, such as the cash flow ratio chart approach developed by Tack[2] for the economic appraisal of numerically controlled machine tools. Kingshott[3] provides a good summary of more specialised techniques, some of which take into account the re-investment opportunities for the repaid capital components during the project life. The application of such techniques, however, transcends the production context and belongs more to the realm of financial management. In this section we shall confine ourselves to some special aspects and applications of the method.

The long construction project. So far we have assumed for the purpose of appraisal that capital expenditure was instantaneous at the beginning of the project period. Bearing in mind the time scale of a substantial project, this assumption is somewhat artificial. The cash outflow often approximates an S curve and with such projects as a new oil refinery or power station the planned time scale of construction will be several years. Late deliveries postpone payments and the cash position can be further affected by project slippage.

Essentially, there are two approaches to this type of proposition. Consider a plant which will take two years to construct and will earn an income for the following eight years. In the first approach everything will be discounted to year 0, the beginning of the project. Subsequent capital expenditures will be discounted just like any other cash flow. The first project benefit will be discounted on a year three instead of a year one basis and later receipts, being in the more distant future, will have corresponding lower present values.

The alternative is to take the project completion date after which the plant revenues are expected to accrue. The project benefits for calendar years three to ten will now be related to an end of year two or beginning of year three base line and then discounted as if they were project years one to eight. On the other hand, all capital expenditures incurred before the end of the year two base line will be *compounded,* not discounted. It is just as if the value of 'i' in our general formula had a minus sign. The discounting base line could be drawn anywhere within a project life; what matters is that the time relationship between capital expenditures and project benefits is properly evaluated.

The discounting time interval. The reader will have noted the convention of the year-end computation of cash flows. This is mainly a matter of convenience and most discount tables are based on this practice. It reflects the end of year accounting approach which verifies cash flow expectations. Some writers prefer mid-year discounting as being more realistic with ongoing operations. Any period could be used for discounting. All it means is that the term 'i' is no longer an integer (whole number). Discount factors can be interpolated from annual tables or worked out from first principles with a pocket calculator.

A more sophisticated approach is continuous discounting. Some companies find it convenient to treat their project benefits on an accruals basis, particularly where monthly operating statements are used for control and decision purposes. A monthly series of project benefits approximates a continuous flow and in such cases continuous discounting techniques are suitable. The summation of discrete benefits, annual lumps of cash, is replaced by the integration of a continuous revenue stream. The notation is that of the calculus of exponential series. The main purpose of this technique is to obtain greater accuracy when large outlays and/or high interest rates are involved. A number of specialist techniques based on this concept of continuous discounting have been well summarised by Massé[4].

Incremental analysis. DCF analysis can form part of an appraisal at any stage of the project preparation process. For instance, it can help in working out the optimum plant size. In some processes there are great economies of scale with the construction of large plants, but we may have to face under-utilisation of capacity. Is it worth it? Incremental analysis can provide a quick answer.

Consider Example No. 1. If we now had an alternative production unit with 20% extra capacity and costing £120000, would this be worthwhile if the net cash flow is lifted by £5000 per annum for the five years? In its simplest form the choice could be represented as in Table 5.8.

Table 5.8

Year	First unit cash flow (£)	Alternative plant cash flow (£)	Incremental values (£)
0	(100000)	(120000)	(20000)
1	40000	45000	5000
2	30000	35000	5000
3	30000	35000	5000
4	25000	30000	5000
5	25000	30000	5000
DCF rate	16.8%		7.9%

We note that the extra investment of £20000 provides a return of 7.9%. Clearly this is not an impressive yield and suggests that the first unit should be chosen.

Incremental analysis has many applications in project

evaluation where variants to a basic proposal are considered, such as with the choice of a process route, replacement problems or the lease/buy decision.

The problem of inflation

Inflation accounting is a contentious business. There is no agreed view as to how inflation should be allowed for in project appraisal. The experience of the last ten years in most countries has been that inflation is a significant, if not serious, factor in the health of a national economy. Its unpredictability is awkward for business calculations but it will not go away just because it is inconvenient. Various cash flow constituents can have different inflation rates; for example, labour costs could rise faster than raw material prices. There are valuation problems and tax complications. What can be done? A number of solutions are offered.

1. One school of thought advocates that project appraisal should ignore inflation. With a long time scale, forecasts are likely to be wrong anyway. The response should be at the operating management level which can adjust prices, plant values and depreciation rates as and when appropriate.
2. An alternative is to index all revenue and cost elements at their expected inflation rates before carrying out the evaluation. With the passage of time the original capital expenditure will look small in current monetary terms and the return on the investment could look disproportionately and misleadingly high.
3. The next approach is to adjust asset values to correspond to current replacement costs. This is not an easy task when there is a great range of specialist equipment supplied in a narrow market and possibly affected by technical change. Nevertheless, in conjunction with method 2, this obviates some of the overstatement of returns related to historical capital costs.
4. Another alternative is to express all future cash flows in

terms of the monetary values as at the evaluation or the capital expenditure stage. Future sales, costs, returns, etc., would all be correspondingly diminished. This might make the prospect more sobering for the evaluators.

5. Finally, a simple device would be to allow for the inflation rate in the minimum acceptable rate of return. For instance, if we take our previous example of a company cut-off rate of 15% and inflation is at 8%, a crude adjustment would be to make the new required rate 23%. This would still, however, underestimate the allowance for inflation. Consider an investment of £100 to be repaid at the end of one year. To maintain the purchasing power of this investment we need to have £108 at the end of the period. Again, the interest payment at the end of the year needs to be maintained in real terms, so this will also have to be multiplied by 1.08. Generally, the adjusted rate of return 'R' with a required real term interest rate 'r' and inflation at 'i'% will be given by the relationship

$$R = r + i \left(1 + \frac{r}{100}\right).$$

$$\text{here} \quad R = 15 + 8 \left(1 + \frac{15}{100}\right) = 24.2\%$$

This general relationship for a given year can be extended over longer periods with (or without) varying inflation rates for different years. The calculation can be further refined by using 'second-order' techniques, such as sensitivity analysis. These will be developed in Chapter 6.

Which of the various solutions to adopt may be a matter of business judgement. One thing is certain; to do nothing about inflation is equivalent to an economic death-warrant. Solutions are not always easy; for instance, a price uplift to maintain revenue in real terms can lead to marketing problems if competitors are underpricing their products because of their unadjusted accounting basis. The first thing a company should endeavour to do is to maintain the real value of its assets and revenues. Its management accounting system, the framework for operational decisions, should use figures which are telling in this respect. Consistency in use comes next, whatever the adopted basis for evaluation and accounting. For example, there must be no manipulation of forecast inflation rates to make a doubtful proposition passable.

Reminder

The appraisal of projects is a quantitative task. The required techniques are well written up in text books and can be readily applied. In doing our calculations, with or without computer, and getting our yields, we might be tempted into smugness and forget how dependent our figures are on the assumptions and expectations of others. A critical approach to every input figure needs to be maintained. Appraisal without audit is mere arithmetic.

Check list: Project evaluation

General

1. Is the project within established policies and objectives?
2. Is the project technically and operationally sound?
3. Who makes the detailed evaluation?
4. Who checks this evaluation?

Specific project aspects

1. What is the basis of project benefit? Cost reduction? Extra contribution from expansion?

2. Have you obtained all *incremental benefits and costs* due to the project?
3. On what basis and assumptions have these been established?
4. Have the specialists responsible for such computations confirmed or endorsed them in writing?
5. What project alternatives have been examined? Different plant sizes, location or processes?
6. What is the horizon, in years, for project calculations?
7. Have all tax allowances and special grants been taken into account?
8. Has the latest corporation tax rate been used in the evaluation of generated project benefits?
9. What provisions have been made for
   a. contingencies,
   b. escalation of project costs,
   c. inflation effects on future operations,
   d. redundancy payments where labour is reduced?
10. What is the required discount rate, net present value, rate of return or payback period? How does the proposal relate to these?
11. What are the main risks of the proposition? Establish the most pessimistic, likely and optimistic combination of circumstances and project outcomes.
12. Have you carried out a sensitivity analysis on the key project parameters?
13. Is the project part of a chain of developments? If so, what are the subsequent decisions that need to be taken?
14. What is the project cash flow pattern? How does it look in a graphical form?
15. What happens if you do not proceed with the project? Are there meaningful alternatives?

References

1. Bromwich, M., *The Economics of Capital Budgeting,* Penguin Books (Harmondsworth, Middlesex, 1976)
2. Tack, A., 'Economic Appraisal', see Leslie, W.H.P., (Ed) *Numerical control users' handbook,* Chapter 4, McGraw-Hill (London, 1970)
3. Kingshott, A.L., *Investment Appraisal,* Ford Business Library (Brentwood, Essex, 1967)
4. Massé, P., *Optimal Investment Decisions,* Prentice-Hall (Englewood Cliffs, N.J., 1962)

Further recommended reading

1. Merrett, A.J., & Sykes, A., *The Finance and Analysis of Capital Projects,* Longmans, (London 1963)
2. Murdick, R.G., & Deming, D.D., *The Management of Capital Expenditures,* McGraw-Hill, (New York, 1968)
3. Wright, R.W., *Investment Decisions in Industry,* Chapman Hall, (London, 1964)
4. Dean, J., *Capital Budgeting,* Columbia University Press, (New York, 1962)

6 Project risk analysis

'Our new automatic plating plant will give us a DCF return of 29.6%.' 'The net present value of the spray shop extension project will be £84640.'

These are splendid, definitive statements. But do they predict what will happen? The somewhat stilted response is usually another question — what do you mean by prediction? Calculation can be blessed with accuracy — that is the property of the concepts we use for such work. It manipulates input data — or 'crunches' it, if you use a computer — irrespective of its fragility. What is the character of such information? Normally it consists, with varying degrees of accuracy, of the 'most likely' estimates from a range of donors — the sales department with product volume projections, the plant engineer (let's hope someone asks him) with expected maintenance and service costs, etc. Sometimes it comes with a word of caution, or a condition/assumption is attached to it. Many an experienced donor builds in a safety margin which may or may not be divulged.

Essentially then, a prediction is a statement as to what is most likely to happen — no more. Putting aside the obvious project disaster when the forecast is patently wrong, we have a single figure without a notion as to the likelihood of that figure being realised. The chances are small that a prediction is precisely met. Apart from the simple replacement project or the 'shopping basket' plant purchase where the variables are few, it might serve management better if it had a range of possible project outcomes over which it can ponder. Better than expected results will always be welcome, but even here it would be nice to know of the possibility beforehand. The risks of shortfall make the case for attention. There are a number of approaches which give management a fuller picture about a proposition than is possible with a single figure calculation. We shall describe the more usable ones.

Some basic methods

These fall into two main categories: (i) those which make explicit allowances for risk although no measure of risk exists; (ii) multi-level evaluations which give a spread of possible project outcomes.

To illustrate how such methods can be applied, take again Example 1 in Chapter 5 (*see* p.104). Here we were concerned with a new production plant at a capital cost of £100000, an expected working life of five years and yielding the net cash flow shown in Table 6.1.

Table 6.1

Year	1	2	3	4	5
Cash flow (£)	40000	30000	30000	25000	25000

Assumed certainty

Here the hazards of the 'most likely' estimate are recognised. Every key value and assumption is scrutinised and adjusted until the analyst is sure that all provisions for uncertainty have been made. For instance, we may have slight doubts whether our equipment costs will be within £100000 but would be quite certain that £130000 will be the limit.

Each factor value is thus taken to the point which contains all possible outcomes the practitioner can possibly envisage; i.e. he is certain that it can't be more, or less, depending on the nature of the factor. In this way he satisfies himself that the project outcome will not be worse.

In a sense, such an approach is similar to the adding of safety factors in engineering design. It is, however, more subjective by nature. The project outcome is now compounded caution which can be related to the initial 'most likely' outcome computation. In our example we could increase capital costs, reduce equipment life and annual cash flows. If our revised yield then came to, say, 12.1% we could state that we are certain our project return will be at least 12.1% and most likely 16.8%.

Risk adjusted rates of return

The required company rate of return is here regarded as a base rate to which a further percentage is added as a form of cover against the risks of the proposition. Again, the added rate is a rather subjective estimate which can vary with different proposition categories. For instance, if in our example the company base rate were 16% and because of the nature of the expected risks there is a rate adjustment of 4%, then our discount rate would amount to 20%. As we can see from our previous calculations this would change the NPV of the project from a gain of £1700 to a loss of £6390, i.e. the project worth does not have sufficient risk cover in this instance.

Three-level evaluations

Three calculations are made, based respectively on the most pessimistic, optimistic and most likely input values. Thus, in our example, as pessimists we could expect our capital costs to be £125000, while in the most fortunate set of circumstances it could be as litle as £85000. Transcribing all project factors on such a basis, we could typically get a return of 12.8% for the most pessimistic, 16.8% for the most likely and 20.2% for the most optimistic project outcome. (A pessimistic estimate is not necessarily assumed certainty.) Thus, the extremities of expectations are defined, giving a spread of possible outcomes within the range. No allowance is, however, made for the likelihood of any particular outcome.

The weighted three-level estimate

This is a composite, weighted development of the previous method. By definition the 'most likely' outcome has a greater chance of being realised and it can be argued that it should be given more weight. A mean outcome value 'r' is computed on the following basis:

$$r = \frac{a + 4m + b}{6}$$

where   a =   optimistic value

b =   pessimistic value

m =   most likely value

The approach is based on the ß (beta) statistical distribution.

Sensitivity analysis

Another way of examining possible variations in project outcome is the application of sensitivity analysis to some of the factors which determine the project yield. Consider the following typical factors with a plant expansion project:

1. Sales volume
2. Selling price
3. Project capital cost

4. Expected plant life
5. Variable operating costs
6. Fixed overhead charges.

After the determination of the single value return rate, based on the 'most likely' values, attention is then concentrated on the range variation of a particular factor, with all other factor values held constant. For instance if, in our example, factor 2, the expected sales price, shows the following variations, resulting in the stated changes of net cash flow (production costs held constant) then the impact on the net present project value is profound, with the minimum required rate of return not being achieved when the sales price is reduced by 4%. We see that the project outcome is very sensitive to variations of this factor. (See Table 6.2.) The procedure may be repeated in respect of each factor, and the sensitivity of the global outcome to the factor under scrutiny can be established. Most likely the various factors will each have a different influence and one of the objects of the method is to establish the key factors which require particularly careful data collection for evaluation purposes. They are also the first candidates for subsequent operational control.

Figure 6.1 illustrates the concept of factor sensitivity. The single value calculation will be at the origin. The vertical axis shows the percentage factor variation from the original value while the horizontal axis indicates variations in project outcome. Line 'a-a' illustrates project sensitivity as well as a direct factor/project value relationship. Line 'b-b' shows an insensitive factor with an inverse relationship, i.e. the lower it is (a cost item), the better the project. The straight lines shown are an approximation. For instance, there could be step functions with some factors, depending on their divisibility.

Some care is required in the use of sensitivity analysis. The presumption that all other factors remain the same, as one particular factor is varied, may remain tenable only for a modest range of the factor itself.

Table 6.2 An example of project outcome variation

Sales price variation	-4%	-2%	0	+2%	+4%
Corresponding project net cash flow variation	-12%	-6%	0	+6%	+12%
Net present project value at 12% (£)	(2,200)	4,500	11,150 (a)	17,950	24,200

(a) given net present value of project on single point estimate.

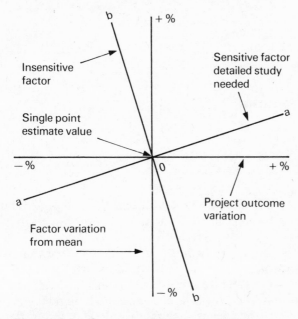

Figure 6.1 Concept of factor sensitivity

Risk analysis

So far, whenever we assessed an investment proposition we used sets of fixed, certain values. This is the *deterministic*

Table 6.3

Year	Cash flow profile 1 Probability = 0.1		Cash flow profile 5 Probability = 0.2	
	Cash flow	Present value	Cash flow	Present value
0	(20000)	(20000)	(26000)	(26000)
1	600	546	1100	1001
2	2000	1660	3200	2656
3	4000	3000	5500	4125
4	5000	3400	8000	5440
5	6000	3720	10000	6200
6	8000	4560	12000	6840
7	6000	3060	11000	5610
8	1500	705	2200	1034
9	1500	630	2200	924
10	234	234	1100	429
Net present values		£1515		£8259

approach. When we no longer accept the complete certainty of a set of figures and introduce the concept of probability, then we are making a *stochastic* evaluation.

The stochastic approach to the investment appraisal is basically concerned with risk. Risk is that part of uncertainty which is amenable to statistical analysis. This presumes sufficient past data for inference and prediction. We are now concerned with the probabilities that the input data or assumptions of the project appraisal may deviate from the expected and result in a different outcome.

With the basic form of risk analysis we first list a set of assumptions and expectations about the project which seem plausible in the light of our knowledge and experience. Each profile could have different capital expenditures and anticipated project benefits. A probability value is then given to each profile which measures the likelihood of that pattern being realised. The probability is anywhere within the range 0 (impossibility) and 1 (certainty). The next step is to work out the worth of each cash flow pattern. Thus we get a series of project values each with a probability coefficient. Multiplying each project value with its coefficient and adding up all products will give us a *mean* project value. This is not the most likely, the *modal* value. They can coincide, but need not. They will, if our probability distribution happens to be symmetrical, such as with a 'normal' distribution.

The following is an example of the approach so far. A plant project with a ten-year life span is assessed on the basis of six different assumptions. The cash flow profile and probability of two of these six are shown. The first is the most pessimistic view and the second is well on the optimistic side. The company discounts its projects at a rate of 10%. In this example the NPVs and their probabilities were as follows:

NPV	PROBABILITY
1515	0.1
4402	0.2
5000	0.2
8259	0.2
4419	0.2
9525	0.1

Multiplying the respective column values we get the mean NPV (u_m) for the project. Thus

$$u_m = 1515 \times 0.1 + 4402 \times 0.2 + 5000 \times 0.2 + \\ 8259 \times 0.2 + 4419 \times 0.2 + 9525 \times 0.1 = £5520$$

In general terms then, the mean project NPV is given by the following formula:

$$u_m = \sum_{i=1}^{i=n} u_i \, p_i$$

where u_i = the NPV of the 'i'th cash flow profile

p_i = the probability of the 'i'th cash flow profile.

The next step in risk analysis is to obtain a statistical measure of the extent of the risk. (A useful background textbook here is Moore's *Principles of Statistical Techniques*[1].) Basically, risk is expressed in terms of the dispersion of likely project outcomes. The bigger the spread, the greater the risk. A first measure of risk is the variance of the project outcome. Variance is a function of the difference between a particular project outcome and the mean project value. In our case the variance is given by 'V' where

$$V = \sum_{i=1}^{i=n} (u_i - u_m)^2 p_i$$

Taking our example

$$V = (1515 - 5520)^2\ 0.1 + (4402 - 5520)^2\ 0.2 +$$
$$(5000 - 5520)^2\ 0.2 + (8259 - 5520)^2\ 0.2 +$$
$$(4419 - 5520)^2\ 0.2 + (9525 - 5520)^2\ 0.1$$
$$= 5.25 \times 10^6\ (\pounds)^2$$

It is now possible to compare this measure of risk with those of other projects. However, the squares of project outcomes are not easily envisaged and a more practical approach is to use the project *coefficient of variation*. This compares the project outcome dispersion with the mean project value. The coefficient of variation 'C' is given by the relationship:

$$C = \sqrt{\frac{variance}{mean}} = \frac{standard\ deviation}{mean}$$

for our case we get:

$$C = \sqrt{\frac{5.25 \times 10^6}{5520}} = \frac{2291}{5520} = 0.415$$

The advantage of this ratio is that it concentrates on the profile, not the scale, of the project values. It avoids the problem where a large project could have a huge variance but still be less risky than a small project with a greater dispersion of project outcomes. We now have a measure of project worth: the NPV of £5520 and a measure of project risk: a coefficient of variation of 0.415.

With such parameters we can compare different projects. The larger the coefficient of variation, the greater will be the risks. Of course, risk works both ways; however, our fears are likely to be riveted by the chances of poor performance. If the coefficient of variation looks too high, it might be better to investigate plant proposals more deeply to reduce the extent of uncertainty.

The promise/risk relationship can readily be shown in graphical form. As we have so far worked in NPV terms, which include an ingredient of project size, we can isolate this by using the project profitability index. You will recall from Chapter 5 that this relates the present value of project benefits to the capital cost of the project. In our example the mean project capital expenditure came to £25000. The profitability index amounts here to $(25000 + 5520)/25000 = 1.221$. Similarly, if we use rates of return we can relate our risk levels directly to these. Figure 6.2 illustrates the relationship.

The ideal project is one well to the right and as close to the X-axis as possible. The top right-hand area has the speculative projects — risky, but rewarding if they come off. The top left-hand side is best left alone. Project A has greater profitability at the same risk level than project B and will, therefore, be preferred. Compared to project C it offers greater worth for greater risk. The trade-off between worth and risk is a matter of judgement and this can vary with decision makers. It is, however, possible to integrate the two aspects with the use of indifference curves: so much risk for so much value, etc. Generally, the use of such illustrations is in the visual aid they supply to judgement and decision making.

One can argue that risk analysis is a lot of work for the insight gained. This may have been true in the past, but with the advent of the desktop computer such a view is no longer tenable. The way in which probabilities are picked is also a matter for debate — the choice has subjective elements but this need not rule it out of court. This important aspect will be further developed in the section commencing on p. 136.

Simulation - the Monte Carlo technique

Of all the stochastic techniques of investment appraisal this has currently the greatest promise. Its strength is based on two factors. Firstly, simulation retains and transcribes the specialist judgements expressed in the probability distribution of any investment input data. There is no need, for the sake of mathematical manipulation, to establish a particular model. Attendant inaccuracies are thus avoided. Secondly, the computer provides a ready tool of analysis for this technique. Simulation gains in effectiveness and meaning when a large number of conditions can be tested. Computer iterations readily provide this.

Although the number of corporate practitioners still seems modest, the method is now well established; see for instance Hertz's account[2]. We shall only be able to outline the main features of this technique.

Sensitivity analysis was concerned with the variation of one project factor, such as capital costs or sales volume, while all the other factors were held constant. Now the project outcome is evaluated with all factors varying simultaneously. For each factor a range of values is considered. Each particular value is given a probability coefficient, again

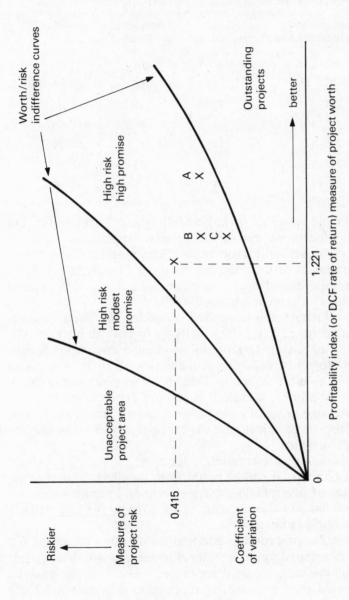

Figure 6.2   Illustration of project worth/risk relationships

Table 6.4 Probability analysis of expected capital costs

Expected capital cost range (£1,000)	Range probability	Cumulative probability	Two-digit values
65 - 75	.01	.01	01
75 - 85	.05	.06	02 - 06
85 - 95	.10	.16	07 - 16
95 - 105	.40	.56	17 - 56
105 - 115	.25	.81	57 - 81
115 - 125	.15	.96	82 - 96
125 - 135	.04	1.00	97 - 00

within the range of 0 (impossibility) and 1 (certainty). On such a basis we can quantify our expectations as to a particular set of factor values. (In practice each factor evaluation is best carried out by those functional managers most experienced and concerned with it. In this manner specialist judgement is utilised.)

To illustrate this approach, consider the plant project, specified on p. 121, which is likely to cost about £100000. Instead of such a single-point estimate a cost range is now given, together with the probabilities of final, alternative costs. These are shown in Table 6.4 and expressed in histogram form in Figure 6.3. It is perhaps easier to assign probabilities to a range of costs rather than to a precise value. For the purpose of calculation the mid-point of a range may be more convenient.

This type of presentation is far more telling than a single point estimate. It will be noted from the illustration that the chances of overspending are greater than keeping within the quoted modal value, or what might become the target figure in the single estimate form.

A similar procedure is adopted for all other major factors and corresponding probability distributions are determined. If, for instance, we used six project factors in our analysis we would then establish six probability distributions. Their

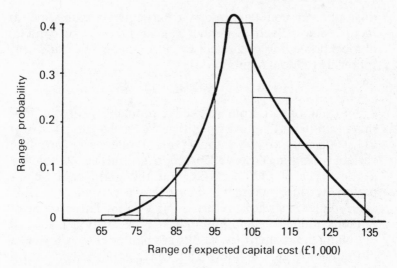

Figure 6.3 Capital cost probability analysis

shapes could be very different; they reflect our factor value likelihood judgements.

The Monte Carlo technique requires the use of random numbers. For this purpose each factor probability distribution is assigned a number of digits. The number of digits chosen indicates the degree of desired accuracy; one digit for ten sub-divisions, two for one hundred sub-divisions. The particular value of each digit set denotes a specific factor value. For instance, if we choose two digits for our factor of expected capital costs and then picked a number at random — 73 — this would be a value in the range of £105 - 115000. If we interpolated within this range our corresponding project cost would be £111 400. It will be noted that digit values are assigned on the basis of equal probability. The weighted factor probability is thus transcribed into digital form - the greater the chance, the bigger the digital range. The total number of digits required will be the product of the factor number and the digit set. In our case, with six factors each allocated two digits, a twelve-digit number could represent a particular combination of factor values. Such a number can be taken from random number tables or generated by a computer. Consider the following random number:

$$73 \quad 43 \quad 59 \quad 42 \quad 23 \quad 86$$

Translating this into our respective probability distributions this could tell us, for example, that we have a capital cost of £111 400, sales of 2000 tons/year, a five-year plant life, variable operating costs at £50/ton, overheads at £40/ton and a sales price of £120/ton, etc. For this given data we, or preferably our computer, work out a corresponding DCF value, either in a rate of return or NPV form. This exercise of random number generation and DCF calculation is carried out many times and if the results are plotted they will yield a histogram of DCF values. This can be transcribed into a probability distribution which represents the interaction of all the factor probability profiles. Figure 6.4 shows a typical example.

The initial project, say scheme A, has a most likely DCF return of 16.7% and in that sense looks more promising than scheme B which can only muster a corresponding return of 12.2%. However, the graph shows a probability of about 0.05 or one in twenty that scheme A could result in a loss. Scheme B, although more modest in expectation, shows no such risk and on that account may be preferable to a management with strong risk aversion.

An alternative form of presentation is in the form of a cumulative probability profile. This is essentially a transcription of Figure 6.4. It will indicate the probability whether a stated return, say 10%, will be achieved or bettered. The probability is given by the proportion of the area contained by the project profile which is to the right of the 10% line. It will be seen that scheme B has a better chance of achieving this. For a return of 20% and above, scheme A has the greater promise.

At first glance, simulation can look somewhat forbidding. It needs a computer for any study in depth. However,

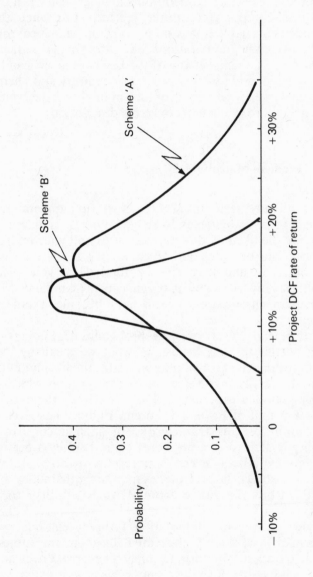

Figure 6.4 Project profitability profile

standard packages are available. If tailor-made programmes are required, the technical/operational manager can enlist the help of his company computer section. But once the programme is available it becomes a valuable analytical tool not only for first computations but also for subsequent developments. A change in any of the key parameters can be quickly assessed, and this very process of quantification helps to discount some of the bias of optimism or pessimism which is more difficult to evaluate from verbal description.

The measurement of probability

We have already seen (pp.125-36) how fundamental the assessment of probabilities is to risk analysis or simulation. Misconceive the likelihood of future events and your refined calculations can be miles out. Even worse, decide on your project objective and keep this in mind when you select probabilities. Any technique or system can be manipulated — when that happens it ceases to be an aid, it becomes a tool for self-deception.

How then can we choose our probabilities? Perhaps it would be better to start by asking what we mean by this term. In lay language, probability indicates the likelihood of an event. It usually involves a forward projection which is based on previous experience. The underlying theoretical framework is that of Bayes's Theorem. Phillips[3] has given a good account of this framework. In such a context a probability is defined as a degree of belief held by a person about some hypothesis, event or uncertain quantity. As we have already shown in previous examples, probabilities are confined within the range from 0 (impossibility) to 1 (certainty).

Our view of the likelihood of a future event has two components. First, there is the past data about the subject matter in question; for instance, machine breakdown and maintenance records. The data can be meagre or extensive, completely to the point or only partially so. Naturally, the more complete and relevant the data the better. The second part is the judgement component which transcribes this input data into a quantified expectation. A subjective view, however good the intuition, is less defensible than 'objective' data, and one would like therefore to see the judgement component as small as possible. But with data incomplete, data at a cost or time-sensitive, and possible discontinuities which affect the extrapolation of past trends, judgement cannot entirely be neglected. This applies particularly to the plant investment decision.

In our case selected probabilities refer either to project factors, such as for simulation, or to project assumptions. The probabilities should be chosen by those who are most experienced in, and have most data about, the behaviour of respective project factors, e.g. the buyer for likely material prices, the sales manager for expected market volume. Thus six project factors may involve six expert opinions.

The task of assigning numerical values begins with the listing of possible alternative outcomes. They could be notionally fixed values or assumptions. Value ranges can also be used. If we take the probability analysis of our capital cost example we have seven such values. We can match each with a probability such that their total amounts to 1 (certainty). To help us visualise our judgement we can put these values on a pie chart as per Figure 6.5

The circle contains what we consider to be all possible outcomes. The various sectors describe our view of the likelihood of a particular event. The larger the area, the greater the angle subtended at the centre, the greater the likelihood. We can then mull over the division and adjust it until we truly feel that it reflects our opinions. The pie chart could also be turned into a spinner to see whether the rest point distribution matched our view of probabilities.

The more distant a future event, the more hazardous seems its prediction. Table 6.5 shows an interesting example where a firm made a prediction of future inflation rates for the purpose of simulation. Hindsight is also given as far as this is

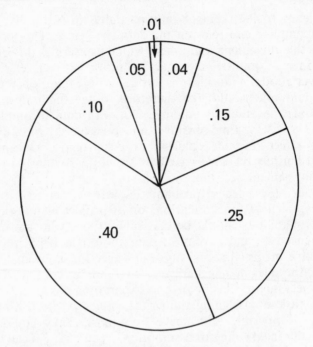

Figure 6.5   Pie chart evaluation of probability

currently available.

It will be noted that the company overstated the inflation rate until 1973 and underestimated it thereafter. If it is remembered that the discounting of future values also reduced their errors, then to some extent these errors seem balanced.

To the working manager the use of probability distributions may seem an unnecessary complication. However a tool of analysis becomes worthwhile when the stake is sufficiently big. They aid the process of decision making if they make the future prospect clearer. Error in assessment has to be seen in context; learning and adjusting at operational level go on. The lack of serious and deep analysis in the first place can at times be much more damaging.

Table 6.5　An inflation forecast made in 1970

	Probabilities of different inflation rates					Weighted forecast %	Actual rates %
	7¾%	10%	11%	12½%	15%		
1970	0.00	0.00	0.00	0.80	0.20	13.00	6.37
1971	0.00	0.00	0.00	0.20	0.80	14.50	9.42
1972	0.00	0.10	0.75	0.15	0.00	11.13	7.11
1973	0.00	0.20	0.50	0.30	0.00	11.25	9.19
1974	0.02	0.25	0.50	0.20	0.03	11.11	16.05
1975	0.02	0.25	0.40	0.30	0.03	11.26	24.26
1976	0.02	0.25	0.40	0.30	0.03	11.26	16.54
1977	0.02	0.25	0.40	0.30	0.03	11.26	15.85
1978	0.02	0.25	0.40	0.30	0.03	11.26	—
1979	0.02	0.25	0.40	0.30	0.03	11.26	—
1980	0.02	0.25	0.40	0.30	0.03	11.26	—

Decision trees

An investment proposition may form part of a series of
decisions which a company may have to make to achieve
long-term objectives. Uncertainty is introduced because the
outcome of subsequent decisions is not yet established, nor
may the behaviour of a key variable, say the intentions of a
major competitor, be readily determined. A number of
techniques exist for such situations, expressed typically in a
tabular or matrix form. They can be used for the calculation,
on the basis of probability assessment, either of a maximum
benefit or minimum loss course, depending on the nature of
optimism/pessimism expressed by the decision makers. The
decision tree method, which illustrates the various stages of a
sequential decision process, can be combined with probability

Table 6.6   Computation of proposition worth

Test result	Decision	Computation	Decision worth (£)
Success	Build 10 000 TPA	$0.6 \times 20\,000 + 0.4 \times 230\,000$	104 000
Success	Build 3 000 TPA	$0.4 \times 50\,000 + 0.6 \times 130\,000$	98 000
Problems	Build 3 000 TPA	$0.4 \times 20\,000 + 0.6 \times 100\,000$	68 000
Problems	Don't build	$0.3 \times (70\,000) + 0.7 \times (20\,000)$	(35 000)
Initial Decision before test	Test process do not test	$0.6 \times 104\,000 + 0.4 \times 68\,000$ $0.4 \times (50\,000) + 0.6 \times 0$	89 600 (20 000)

Figures in brackets are losses.

assessment to determine the outcome of a number of alternative courses open to a firm. Consider the case of a firm which is faced with the decision whether to test a new process and whether to build a new production unit. Figure 6.6 shows the method:

In this case the company has two major risks to contend with:
1. The possible failure of its test programme
2. The intentions of a major competitor.

It expresses its judgement about these risks in probability terms. The risks are sequentially related and there is a time-lag between the two outcome categories. Also, the second risk profile is affected by the second category of decisions. The decision tree lists all the outcomes that are feasible in a given situation. The financial benefit of each outcome is calculated so as to present the decision makers with a full spectrum of promise and risk. The analyst then obtains the value of alternative courses of action by multiplying the worth of an outcome by its probability. This gives the computation shown in Table 6.6.

The computation is a backward calculation. The final outcomes are transcribed into intermediate outcome equivalents. Related to a decision, the better outcome equivalents will then be chosen. Thus, with decision 2a the

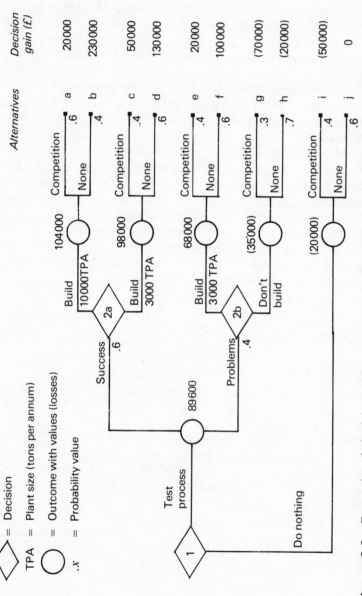

Figure 6.6   Example of decision tree approach: investment in a new process and plant

benefit of building the 10000 TPA plant (£104000) is greater
than building the 3000 TPA unit (£98000). Decision 2a will
then be to build the large plant. In turn, this decision value
will be integrated into decision 1. The outcome values in
respect of this decision tell us to test the process. Our overall
decision programme then will be to test the process and, if
successful, to build the large plant. If there are test problems
then, with our given outcome spectrum, a small plant should
be built.

No one would deny the hazards of sequential prediction,
particularly if there are a number of decision stages. The
value of the technique is not in a precise specification of a
particular monetary outcome; it is mainly in the listing of all
possible alternatives and their systematic evaluation. In a
decision context the importance is in the relative merits of
different courses of action. Because of this the decision tree
approach, although known as an appraisal technique, is also
relevant to the project preparation stage.

Other techniques

This chapter has described some basic techniques of risk
analysis. There is more. There is the analysis of interrelated
projects, of project portfolios and project time series. Such
techniques require the building of mathematical models.
They belong to the field of operational research and are
beyond the scope of this book. Applications of utility theory
have also been omitted. Readers who wish to explore these
areas are advised to consult some of the further reading
references.

References

1. Moore, P.G., *Principles of Statistical Techniques,* Cambridge University Press, (Cambridge, 1969)
2. Hertz, D.B., *New Power for Management,* McGraw-Hill, (New York, 1969)
3. Phillips, L.D., *Bayesian Statistics for Social Scientists,* Nelson, (London, 1973)

Further reading

1. Canada, J.R., *The Consideration of Risk and Uncertainty in Capital Investment Analyses,* Management International Review, 1967/6, Betriebswirtschaftlicher Verlag Dr. Th. Gabler (Wiesbaden, 1967)
2. Carter, C.F., Meredith, G.P. and Shackle, G.L.S., *Uncertainty and Business Decisions,* Liverpool University Press, (Liverpool, 1962)
3. Hanssmann, F., *Operations Research Techniques for Capital Investment,* J. Wiley, (New York, 1968)
4. Hillier, F.S., *The Evaluation of Risky Interrelated Investments,* North-Holland Publishing Co., (Amsterdam, 1969)
5. Rose, L.M. *Engineering Investment Decisions,* Elsevier Scientific Publishing Co., (Amsterdam, 1976)
6. Townsend, E.C., *Investment and Uncertainty,* Oliver and Boyd, (Edinburgh, 1969)
7. Wright, W.R., *Investment Decisions in Industry,* Chapman Hall, (London, 1964)

7 Plant replacement

To an engineer with a sense of history, it is a marvellous experience to see a beam engine, over one hundred years old, still working on a productive task. To an economist it looks odd that such a quaint piece of machinery is still in use.

These views represent extremities of opinion. With a going concern and established products, much of new plant investment is in fact replacement. Modernisation brings new processes, techniques and equipment. Out goes the old plant, and with it experience, know-how made obsolescent, and many years of association between man and machine which influence the climate and organisation of the work place. Our concern in this chapter is with the operational and economic aspects of plant replacement. But let the context be acknowledged. Ever since the Industrial Revolution, perhaps history's most significant period of plant replacement, the introduction of new equipment has social, economic and political repercussions. The arena itself has not changed even if the balance of power within it has somewhat altered. The reader should therefore bear in mind the social and behavioural aspects of change with some forms of plant replacement: the bargaining and tactical opportunities these represent; the disappointments and frustrations that may ensue. The industrial manager has to live with this context — plant replacement does not take place in a vacuum.

After this reminder let us concentrate on the task before

us. First we are concerned with the concept and character of the plant replacement decision. Next comes the concept of operating inferiority which integrates the effects of plant deterioration and obsolescence. Various plant replacement models are developed. Finally 'repair' is considered as an alternative to 'replace'.

The character of the plant replacement decision

In essence, plant replacement occurs when a machine is removed from its operational function and another takes its place. The operational function of a machine is the job it has to carry out. It might have been designed for that very purpose. Alternatively, the operation might be part of a broad range of work to which it can be applied. Of course, the versatility of the machine can very much affect its fate subsequent to the replacement.

Let us consider further this concept of operational function. Normally a piece of equipment is bought against a supplier's specification. He holds out what a machine can do in a given set of circumstances. These are the *design conditions*. A responsible plant supplier builds in a safety margin to ensure that his undertaking is met in contract. He couples this with advice and cautions about the operation and maintenance of the equipment, this reflecting his own experience and that of previous clients. An alert production staff can often find ways of unlocking such a margin and improving on the design conditions. For example, with the aid of such techniques as evolutionary operation it can squeeze extra output from the plant. Thus, under carefully defined conditions and possibly with minor modifications it can achieve *best operating conditions*. These can be an appreciable advance on the supplier's specification.

After a period of operation plant performance begins to decline or is maintained only at a much greater support cost. A lower limit of *minimum operating standards* is reached below which the plant is considered for replacement. This reflects the simplest, static position where minimum conditions are well defined and long established. The mix of factors which underlies our view about operating performance also forms a basis for the plant replacement review.

Factors in the replacement review

The simplest approach is to argue that a machine is unsafe and/or uneconomic to operate and therefore it needs to be replaced. If the first part of the sentence were true, the deduction still is not bound to follow and the costs of replacement could, in any case, warrant closer scrutiny of the case. What aspects need to be considered? We need not take a major plant failure where the dimensions of disaster speak for themselves. We are more concerned with the accumulation of minor costs and disadvantages which gradually tilt the scale against an incumbent machine. The worth of a production plant can be seen in terms of input/output analysis. The output is a finished or intermediate product with a certain value. The greater the inputs required for a given output, the less effective is the machine.

Increasing unit costs of production. In its simplest form this can be due to a loss of production. The fixed equipment and attendance costs are carried by fewer units of output. Various reasons can be advanced for this. Most common is increased downtime; stoppages are more frequent, setting up a machine run takes longer, etc. A higher grade of labour or material may have to be used to maintain previous performance levels.

Declining operating efficiencies. This trend is often due to lower operating speeds so that the specified quality levels can be maintained. Alternatively, higher scrap or rework rates have to be accepted. In the process industries, batch yields may diminish or utilities consumptions increase per unit of output.

Rising maintenance costs. Plant deterioration is a function of use and age. An ageing plant can result in more breakdowns and bigger overhauls. More spares need to be carried and with time they will be increasingly difficult to get.

Change in work mix. Here the usability of output becomes the main consideration. As production requirements change — and we are concerned here with longer-term trends — the particular set of facilities incorporated in a machine are no longer required. The plant is redundant.

Obsolescence. Here the machine input/output pattern is related to competitive equipment, embodying different technologies. The production requirement may be the same but the means of achievement, and their economics, have changed.

Health and safety. A production unit can become unsafe as it ages, or an unsuspected risk is disclosed by an accident. Replacement can also be considered, not because of an inherent change in the equipment, but because of a change in awareness and attitudes. In the United Kingdom, the Health and Safety at Work Act 1974 and greater knowledge about industrial diseases have contributed to this.

Constituents of the replacement review

Our concept of the plant replacement process indicates that it consists of a number of sub-decisions. They can be readily presumed but in effective decision making they are explicit. They are most telling in the form of questions:

Which plant is to be removed? It may be the sole plant item or one of many. A given plant item may ostensibly be on its own, but its function could be taken over by a different machine. There are substitution possibilities: say, a turret lathe could do work assigned normally to a centre lathe. Where a group of similar machines is in operation, such as with a weaving or knitting unit in the textile industry, this question may be resolved by standard practice rather than a *de novo* analysis.

Should it be replaced? With a given production process, plant replacement is normally presumed. Nevertheless, a process/ecnomic review at this stage may discover meaningful alternatives. A given set of equipment is a form of constraint; it fixes the basic context for the decision maker. He can break out of this, but at a cost, either by sub-contracting work or investing in a new plant. Now is the moment of flexibility, to look again at first principles. Alternative process routes could make the replacement unnecessary, or it might be more economic to buy in from specialist suppliers. To assume replacement is automatic could be an opportunity lost.

What should replace it? Here the promise or, preferably, the attainments of alternative equipment will be assessed and related to the performance of the existing plant. *Pure replacement* means that an identical machine takes the place of the existing unit. The possibility of this diminishes with the length of plant life. Such replacements may be desirable where plant life is very short or it is important to maintain a given operating practice. However, in most cases plant replacement is an opportunity to incorporate the following:

1. *Technical change,* i.e. the latest proven practices.
2. *Changes in the functional specification* such as a different range of speeds or work size, accessories, such as loading or unloading devices.
3. *Changes in the scale of operation.* Incidentally, the replacement need not be a new plant item in the commercial sense.

When to replace? In practice, the decision not to replace is a deferment to the next review period. The timing of the replacement decision can be critical not only in terms of existing plant performance but also in relation to current and prospective technical developments. This is well illustrated by

Terborgh's[1] concept of operating inferiority which will be developed in the next section.

What should be done with the replaced equipment? If there is enough space nothing needs to be done — the cost of dismantling is saved; the machine stays in place, sometimes as a reminder of busier times. This 'petrification' of production plant can sometimes be seen in old-established but declining sections of British industry. However, there is a more positive argument for leaving some machines *in situ*. They are available as standby plant should the new equipment need overhaul or in case of breakdown. Equipment which has few moving parts or is not all that different from the current technology is suitable for such a role, e.g. boilers, centrifugal pumps, etc. There is a third alternative, the machine stays put and is given another function, usually of a less exacting nature. Plant replacement is here first as a substitution in function; physical removal is common, but not always a necessary consequence.

However, in the absence of such alternatives, a sense of good housekeeping or space needs usually prompt management to remove the replaced equipment. In such cases three choices are available:

1. *Scrapping of plant*
   The plant is sold for its material value. In some instances, such as with non-ferrous process vessels, this is by no means negligible. Often the price of the old equipment is equated to the cost of breaking up and removal carried out by the purchaser. Scrapping a plant can also include the deliberate destruction of systems or components, lest they should find other operational or commercial uses after disposal.

2. *Resale*
   This can be in the open market as second-hand equipment either at home or abroad. Sales can also be to associated companies when they may form part of a transaction which goes far beyond plant disposal.

3. *Allocation to another function*

A machine may start its career on high quality work, say in a toolroom, then be transferred to standard production, and finish its life in the apprentice workshop. The functional task becomes less exacting with time. Terborgh describes such 'easing up' as functional degradation.

In other cases a plant can move within a large manufacturing group from one factory to another as part of corporate operations management or following discovery in the company surplus plant bulletin.

Repair or replace? This is really a specific aspect of the decision constituent discussed on p.147. As we shall see later in the chapter, repair need not be just the restoration of a plant item to its original state. An overhaul can be used to incorporate plant innovations.

The concept of operating inferiority

The concept of operating inferiority is an important aspect of replacement analysis. The urge for equipment replacement often comes from the plant engineer, the person most aware of the physical deterioration of production plant. This is an important, but an in-house stimulus. What goes on elsewhere, outside the firm, may not get enough attention. Terborgh counters such a partial view. At any time we should compare what we have in our factories with the very latest proven equipment which is available to us and to our competitors. The difference in performance between our ageing, incumbent plant and that of the latest equipment — the challenger — is the operating inferiority of our equipment. How can this difference be measured? It can be stated in terms of contribution: the difference in value produced and costs incurred. Alternatively, it can be expressed in cost effective terms; the unit costs incurred in producing a given article. Figure 7.1 gives an example of the concept of

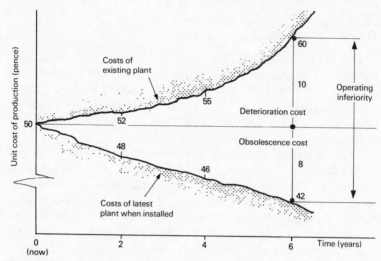

Figure 7.1 The concept of operating inferiority

operating inferiority. For the purpose of illustration we have neglected inflation, although transcription into constant cost terms would not be difficult. We have also ignored any initial running-in costs which might be experienced with new plant.

Figure 7.1 shows two unit cost curves. The existing plant costs rise with deterioration over time. The growth of obsolescence is shown by the reducing unit cost curve of the latest equipment at the date of purchase. The two relative cost components, deterioration and obsolescence, together make up operating inferiority. It is the gap between the two curves at any moment in time which is significant.

Imagine you have just installed a new piece of equipment, giving you a unit production cost of 50p. Because of wear, unit production costs in, say, two years' time will be 52p. If you had delayed your purchase for two years and then bought the latest model available, then your unit costs would be 48p. The gap between your actual costs and the lowest possible costs (other things equal) will be 52-48 = 4p per unit. Similarly, at the end of four years the gap would be 9p and after six years 18p per unit. The gap is then accounted for by:

(a) 10p of unit deterioration costs.
(b)   8p of unit obsolescence costs.

The actual pattern of the curves will vary with plant and industry. The steeper they are, the faster is deterioration and technical change. Full obsolescence is reached when technical change is such that the old plant — whatever its physical condition — is uneconomic to operate in a given competitive situation.

The concept of operating inferiority is valuable as such but it needs hard figures to make it useful for operational decisions. The deterioration component can be estimated from plant maintenance and output records. A good record system is required and its cost needs to be justified. The challenge is in the forecast of the obsolescence factor. In some cases it may be possible to foretell dramatic changes. For instance, once the promise of semiconductors was realised the scope of application could be envisaged. But even where advances are not so telling, projections are possible. Companies with ongoing cost reduction programmes often manage to improve production processes by many little refinements which become important as they accumulate with time. Experience can be built up to form the backcloth of judgement about future trends. Prediction here involves the specialists and uses the techniques of technological forecasting.

So what is the point of the concept? Its purpose is to ensure the correct timing of the replacement decision. The objective is the minimisation of capital costs and operating inferiority costs. The latter is the unit excess cost multiplied by the volume of production. Frequent replacement so as to be technically up-to-date means heavier capital costs, while the shorter machine life will reduce the level of return. With infrequent replacements the burden of operating inferiority tells on trading margins. So a balance needs to be struck; the next section shows how this can be done.

Some plant replacement models

The purpose of models is to provide decision rules for meaningful, consistent analysis. They incorporate objective functions which are to be maximised (profits) or minimised (costs). In the production management context cost minimisation is generally the more useful approach.

Before illustrating various rules we need to remind ourselves of the nature of the trade-off involved. Whenever we invest in a piece of equipment we have capital costs which need to be recovered. The longer the expected equipment life, the lighter will be the annual capital charge. The lump sum of capital expenditure is spread over a longer time scale. Against this we have increases in running costs as the plant ages, such as lower efficiencies, greater maintenance expense, etc. Let us call all these costs *support costs,* as they are the costs incurred in the support of the machine in its functional role. Repair and general maintenance are often the major part but not the sum total of support costs. Again, the purpose of our models is to minimise the total of our annual capital and support costs.

The support cost limit

This specifies that when support costs reach a certain fraction of the original plant capital cost (adjusting for inflation) the machine is replaced.

Consider a machine which has a net capital cost of £10000 and no resale/salvage value. Its annual support costs are as follows:

Year	Support costs (£)
1	500
2	1000
3	1500
4	2500
5	3000
6	4000

Table 7.1

Year	1	2	3	4	5	6
Annual support cost	500	1000	1500	2500	3000	4000
Average support cost for machine life	500	750	1000	1375	1700	2083
Annual capital cost if replaced at end of year	10000	5000	3333	2500	2000	1667
Total annual average cost	10500	5750	4333	3875	3700	3750

If the *annual support cost limit* were, say, 30% of the capital cost, then the machine would be replaced in year five. Alternatively, we could specify a *cumulative support cost limit,* for instance 50% of capital cost. In this case we would replace in year four, the year in which the running total costs reach £5000. This type of rule is simple but not very effective as no allowance is made for the capital cost of replacement.

Minimum average annual capital and support costs (£)

Taking the same example we obtain the results shown in Table 7.1. In this model the machine is best replaced at the end of year five, when we have the lowest combined annual cost of £3700. If it is possible that we can resell the machine on the second-hand market, say, we have a fork lift truck, we can allow for this by incorporating resale values in our model.

Plant support and capital cost pattern with plant resale values(£)

In this case the lowest annual cost if £3250 and the machine is best replaced at the end of year four. Table 7.2 shows that re-sale values could in certain industries affect the economic

Table 7.2

Year	1	2	3	4	5	6
Year end resale value	6000	4500	3000	2500	1500	500
Capital cost to date	4000	5500	7000	7500	8500	9500
Capital cost per year	4000	2750	2334	1875	1700	1583
Average support cost for plant life	500	750	1000	1375	1700	2083
Total annual average cost	4500	3500	3334	3250	3400	3660

plant life span. Models such as the last two described can be further developed to include other cost variables - the principle is the same. Taxation adjustments can also be included.

The general case for this type of replacement model can be expressed as follows:

let E = expense function to be minimised
   C = net capital cost of plant replacement
  $S(n)$ = expected resale/salvage value at end of period 'n'
   f_i = plant support cost in the 'i'th period
   n = number of periods

Then E is given by the relationship

$$E = C + \sum_{i=1}^{i=n} f_i - S(n)$$

This overall cost can be transcribed to a period basis 'e' where $e = E/n$. Generally, the minimum cost level occurs when the incremental support costs increase at a rate which equals the savings in annual capital costs due to the extended machine life.

The discounted capital and support cost pattern

This is similar in principle to the previous models except that the time value of costs is now also considered.

let r = rate of interest

The present value (PV) of the expense function will be given by:

$$E(PV) = C + \sum_{i=1}^{i=n} \left[\frac{f_i}{(1+r)^i} \right] - \frac{S(n)}{(1+r)^n}$$

The present value approach is useful when plant replacement is related to other courses of action such as a major plant overhaul. Let us take our initial example and examine it on a present value of cost basis. The present value of costs for a given machine life cycle will be the initial plant investment together with the present value of future support costs. It will be noted from the example that lower discount factors reduce the higher annual support costs in the more distant future. Nevertheless, the longer the machine life span, the greater will be the total present value costs. But when this is expressed in equivalent annual instalments these diminish as the machine life is extended. An interest rate of 10% is used in Table 7.3.

Consider a four-year plant life, i.e. replacement after four years. To meet the support cost as given over the four years, taking the time value of money at 10%, we need to provide four end-of-year instalments of £1297. Similarly, to recover our initial plant outlay of £10000 over this period we have to find £3150 each year, giving a total annual sum of £4447. It will be noted that the lowest annual instalment cost will be with a machine life of 6 years — the limit of our forecasting horizon in this example.

With this approach the time pattern of support costs is

Table 7.3 Discounted plant support and capital cost pattern (£)

Year service	Annual support costs	Discount factor at 10%	Present value of support cost	Cumulative PV of support cost	Annuity factor at 10%	Support cost instalment	Capital cost instalment	Total annual equivalent
1	500	0.909	455	455	1.100	500	11000	11500
2	1000	0.826	826	1281	0.576	738	5760	6498
3	1500	0.751	1127	2408	0.402	968	4020	4988
4	2500	0.683	1708	4116	0.315	1297	3150	4447
5	3000	0.621	1863	5979	0.264	1578	2640	4218
6	4000	0.564	2256	8235	0.230	1894	2300	4194

Annuity factor at 10%, year x $= \dfrac{1}{\text{Sum of 10\% discount factors to year x}}$

important and can determine with what equipment to replace. Other variables, such as changes in the resale/salvage value, can readily be included in the model.

The MAPI approach

This form of replacement analysis was developed by Terborgh[2] and published by MAPI, the Machinery and Allied Products Institute. Its primary purpose in a given production context is to decide whether to replace plant or whether to defer such a decision for another year. It focuses on the operating inferiority of the incumbent machine, the 'defender', in relation to the best which is currently available — the 'challenger'. The operating inferiority of the defender is the operating advantage of the challenger. The first task of the method is to calculate this for the next year. This consists of all the incremental operating benefits which accrue from replacement: typically, increased output, savings in labour costs, downtime, maintenance, etc. Terborgh also adds notional values for such intangibles as safety and flexibility.

After this he considers the non-operating advantages of the replacement. This establishes the capital costs avoided if the old machine were sold now compared to a year's time. The total challenger advantage is then obtained by addition. This, Terborgh maintains, will also be the defender's adverse minimum. With his assumption that operating inferiority increases at a constant rate — leaving the replacement for another year will make the gap between the two units just that much bigger — there is no need to consider subsequent years.

Next, Terborgh looks at the challenger. The growth of operating inferiority goes on. The successful challenger, now ensconced in the functional role, is not exempt from the competition of future challengers some years hence. How long will its tenure be in that role? This is an important question because it will affect the very strength of the challenge now under scrutiny. The shorter the expected challenger life, the greater is its annual burden of capital cost and the corresspondingly weaker will be its challenge.

Take our previous example and assume that our existing machine A is four years old. A replacement unit B shows a total advantage for year five of £5000. This will be machine A's adverse minimum. Unit B's net investment cost is £22000. The challenger B will in turn accumulate operating inferiority in relation to a future machine C at a rate of £1000 per annum. We then work out machine B's expected working life on the basis of discounted operating inferiority and capital costs. The calculation is the same as our previous example, except that we replace support costs by operating inferiority. (Terborgh is concerned with relative gain, not absolute reults. Support costs would in any case feature as a component of operating inferiority.) In the end we find our minimum annual instalment costs which give us the expected working life of challenger B. This minimum instalment rate is the *challenger's* adverse minimum (against future unit C). If this were, say, £4000, i.e. less than defender A's adverse minimum, then the replacement should take place.

Terborgh supports this approach with a set of forms and charts which simplify evaluation. These allow for various tax, capital consumption (depreciation) patterns, salvage ratios, etc. The forms are designed to give a project urgency rating — the greater the gap between defender A's and challenger B's adverse minima, the greater is the urgency rating. Urgency is expressed as a percentage figure of the proposed investment. These are not the absolute returns on the project because in the calculation of instalment costs there is already a discount factor equivalent to the interest cost of the money used. However, they provide the necessary project ranking where a number of projects compete for limited funds.

The value of the MAPI approach is perhaps more in its concept than in its computation. It encourages a systematic annual review of existing plant which looks as much at outside developments as at machine performance. The assumption of linear increases in operating inferiority over a long forecasting horizon is not easily defended. But as Terborgh himself maintains, investment formulae are an aid to judgement, not its substitute.

The 'repair or replace' decision

The 'repair or replace' problem is mainly faced by plant engineers or plant managers, i.e. at the operations management level. Where the problem is due to sudden plant failure, decision making is under pressure. Part of the stress then arises when a plant manager has to ask his board for heavy, unexpected capital expenditure. Perhaps there is no choice; but often there is and the line of least organisational resistance then points to improvisation. Thus the day of reckoning can be postponed.

Operational pressures often run the life of the plant engineer. He finds it difficult to stand back and take a detached view about the 'repair/replace' decision. Where the breakdown is not of the fatal kind, 'repair' is like a reflex action and over the years a skill and record of achievement is built up which shows the ingenuity of a plant department, usually working with very limited resources.

We have already considered what is meant by 'replace' and before going further we need to do the same for 'repair'.

Repair is to restore an item to an acceptable condition by the renewal, replacement or mending of decayed or damaged parts. (B.S.3811 : 1974, Glossary of Maintenance Terms in Terotechnology)

The acceptable plant condition which a repair aims to achieve may be the operational specification or one given by the original supplier. The actual condition of the plant prior to the repair-need stage could be above this level. A repair may reinstate such condition or, falling short of this, still reach the minimum required state of plant.

It will also be noted that a repair is a composite activity including the replacement of parts. The borderline between 'repair' and 'replace' can be fine when repair includes the large-scale replacement of parts. Normally, if the main equipment structure remains intact the term 'repair' applies.

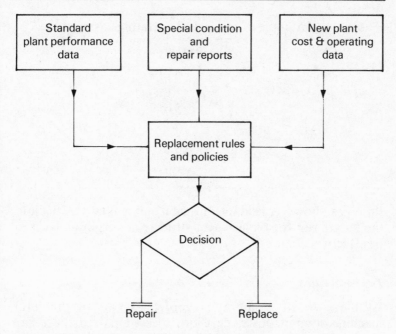

Figure 7.2 A simplified repair/replace decision system

The inputs to the repair/replace decision

A decision based on no information is at best a gamble. A management information system needs to provide standard data which enables a plant manager to monitor the performance of existing equipment and to predict its future state. Specific reports supplement the information for the particular decision, such as machine condition, repair costs, parts availability, subsequent operational performance, etc. All this input can then be evaluated against given decision/ policy rules and an alternative chosen. The process can be shown in a simplified form by Figure 7.2.

As with most companies the 'repair/replace' decision is relatively infrequent, the data system and decision rules tend not to be developed. *Ad hoc* decisions, made in their absence, need not necessarily be wrong in a given case. Such improvi-

Table 7.4 Example of repair and operating cost patterns

Choice →	Repair costs	New machine
	£4000	*£10000*
Future operating costs	*Repaired machine*	*New unit*
Year 1	£2000	£300
2	£2500	£400
3	£3000	£500
4	£3500	£800

sation can however lead to confusion and makes it difficult in the longer run for replacement strategy at corporate level to be effective.

Decision rules

As the costs of repair are regarded as part of the total machine support costs, decision rules similar to those for plant replacement can be applied. We can use *annual repair limits* and/or cumulative repair limits. In the absence of other support costs we can similarly minimise average annual capital and repair costs. The following approaches are also helpful in the repair/replace decision situation.

Minimum present cost models. The models can be applied to the analysis of major repair jobs, i.e. where the cost of a particular repair would be a significant fraction of the plant replacement cost. Obviously, as the two costs come closer the case for repair diminishes. The problem is where to draw the line. From a purely economic point of view the lowest present value of both repair/replacement and future operating costs should be chosen. Take the example of a repair job on a machine tool. The repair costs less than the replacement but the machine is not as good as new, i.e. its operating costs are higher.

In Table 7.4 the new machine costs 2.5 times the amount of

Table 7.5 Present value of cost patterns

Year	Discount factor (15%)	Present value cost flow repaired unit	Present value cost flow new unit
0	1.00	£4000	£10000
1	0.87	1740	261
2	0.76	1900	304
3	0.66	1980	330
4	0.57	1995	456
Total present value of costs		£11615	£11351

repairs but shows significant savings. If we assume that the company has to pay 15% for the use of money, then the respective present value costs are given by Table 7.5. The present cost value of a new machine is lower and the replacement should be carried out.

Incremental analysis. Again, this approach is suitable for major repairs. Instead of comparing overall cost structures it concentrates on incremental costs. In this respect it is similar to the standard form of plant investment analysis using the

Table 7.6 Incremental analysis using previous data

Extra investment for new machine	(£)	Discount factor at 15%	Present value of cash flow (£)
	(6000)	1.00	(6000)
Savings in operating costs Year 1	1700	0.87	1479
Year 2	2100	0.76	1596
Year 3	2500	0.66	1650
Year 4	2700	0.57	1539
Net present value (NPV)			£264

discounted cash flow (DCF) technique. Its operation is illustrated (see Table 7.6) using the previous data. In this case the company more than recovers its investment and receives a return of 15%.

If the net present value had been negative then the savings would have been insufficient for the outlay and the repair should have been carried out.

Stochastic replacement models

These are replacement models which use probability distributions for plant failure and repair cost predictions. This interesting subject is unfortunately beyond the scope of this book, but interested readers may wish to make separate studies of the main topics.

The dynamic programming approach to repair limits

The main exponent of this is Hastings[3]. It is most suitable for equipment with a relatively limited service life and which requires annual inspections and overhauls. Typical applications include fleets of trucks or road tankers, civil engineering plant or oil exploration equipment. The annual inspection provides an estimate of overhaul costs. The technique specifies the rules whether the plant should be overhauled or replaced. It gives the repair cost limits for different equipment ages and for different future periods within a set planning horizon. The rules are based on probability distributions of overhaul costs and take into account plant age, useful remaining service life and resale values. The purpose of the technique is to minimise total repair and replacement costs for the given planning period.

Dynamic programming is a fairly sophisticated technique. Its application, which requires systematic and accurate cost data, can only be justified if a large number of expensive plant items are involved.

Component replacement models

This is an allied subject area to plant replacement. A number of techniques exist and these are usually contained within the topic of reliability engineering. Essentially, they deal with the failure of components or sub-systems which stop plant operation. Failure patterns are established in probability terms and various strategies of preventive replacement as against failure replacement are examined. Much depends on the cost of replacing — as distinct from the cost of the item involved — as plant downtime costs become important. A number of writers have developed this subject and their contributions are listed for further reading.

Check list: Plant replacement

NOTE: This list is an extension of the check list on project preparation and should be used in conjunction with it.

1. Take at random one of your production units — what does it cost to maintain?
2. Are you satisfied with the maintenance cost recording and reporting system?
3. What are the downtime losses in your production departments? What are the main causes?
4. How does your plant range relate to the work mix of your order book?
5. If a factory inspector were to call tomorrow, which piece of equipment would embarrass you most? Why? What will you do about it?
6. How does your plant compare with the best in use?
7. What technical developments are most likely to affect your present plant; which machines in particular?
8. What plant replacement criteria do you use? What are the decision rules?
9. Who makes the plant replacement decisions?

10. Do you have a plant replacement programme?
11. Do you work out the gain expected from the replacement plant?
12. How do you ensure that the quoted gain is achieved?
13. Have you evaluated all the direct and indirect effects of plant replacement on the shop floor? What will the effects be on plant services, operations, maintenance, manning, incentive schemes, pay packets, etc.?

References

1. Terborgh, G., *Dynamic Equipment Policy,* McGraw-Hill, (New York, 1949)
2. Terborgh, G., *Business Investment Policy,* Machinery & Allied Products Institute, (Chicago, 1958)
3. Hastings, N.D.Y., *The Repair Limit Replacement Method* Operational Research Quarterly, *20,* 337, (London, 1969)

Additional reading

1. Connor, J. and Evans, J.B., *Replacement Investment,* Gower, (London, 1972)
2. Arinc Research Corporation, *Reliability Engineering,* Prentice-Hall, (Englewood Cliffs, N.J., 1964)
3. Ireson, W., *Reliability Handbook,* McGraw-Hill, (New York, 1966)
4. Jardine, A.K.S., *Maintenance, Replacement and Reliability,* Pitman, (London, 1973)
5. Jorgenson, D.W., McCall, J.J. and Radnor, R., *Optimal Replacement Policy,* North-Holland Publishing Co., (Rotterdam, 1967)

8 Plant leasing

Production managers, plant engineers and related operational staff are primarily concerned with the effective and economic operation of production plant. Details of ownership, as such, are not the first consideration in the operational context. Yet it is production needs which generate investment proposals. Authorisation of these submissions presumes appropriate financial arrangements for the plant to be acquired. In most cases straight purchase is the obvious route. Yet there are limits to this. The company's cash resources may be inadequate for a plant investment programme and other forms of finance have to be found. Leasing the asset could be one of several practical alternatives and it might be better to have this than to do without the required equipment.

Apart from financial aspects there are, at times, important operating reasons for plant leasing. Some equipment, such as computers, have become very specialised and sophisticated. Quite apart from the problems of maintenance which might have to be contracted out in any case, there are risks of obsolescence and change in user requirements.

There has been rapid growth in equipment leasing in recent years. For instance, the Equipment Leasing Association, in its annual report, June 1977, indicates that the assets leased by its members have increased threefold over the last five years. The total value of plant and machinery held by its members on lease amounted to £753 million on the 31 December 1977. This represented 64833 different contracts with a mean lease value of £11614. As leases normally run for a number of years this mean value tends to reflect historic costs. Considering the 1977 figures on their own, the average lease contract in that year amounted to £21000 and the total assets value acquired by members came to £198 million. The category of plant and machinery was the most important by value, being followed in 1977 by computer and office equipment, commercial vehicles and cars. Excluding agricultural equipment, plant and machinery constituted 29.3% by value of the total leasing business for 1977. Some of the production plant included in this figure consists of machine tools, printing presses, textile machinery, boot and shoe machinery, generators, pumps, boilers and contractor's plant.

The growing importance of leasing has also been emphasised by Sykes[1] in his survey of the lease/buy decision as reflected in the practice of 202 member companies of the British Institute of Management. Sykes gives three major reasons for the growth of leasing. The first is concerned with the United Kingdom system of corporate taxation where investment incentives come in the form of capital allowances to be set against taxable profits. A fast-growing or capital-intensive business may not have sufficient taxable profits to utilise the allowances and, subject to appropriate terms, it might be better to have an immediate though indirect use of such allowances via a lease rather than wait for profits to reach the required level. The second major reason is that leasing provides an *extra* source of funds for a business. The firm does not commit its own capital funds and this is important where business opportunities are expanding faster than financial resources. Other important advantages relate to capital gearing and aspects of disclosure. The third important reason relates to cash flow and budgeting. When the investment is large in relation to the customary business level, leasing helps to smooth cash flows and aids budgetary control, especially where maintenance is the lessor's responsibility.

Basic leasing concepts

Before considering the nature of the lease/buy decision it is useful to clarify a number of terms in common use with leasing practice. In the first place a *lease* is a contract where one party obtains the use of equipment owned by another. For this use it pays a rental. The *lessor* owns the equipment and grants a lease on it. The *lessee* is the user of the leased plant. In practice, within the term 'lease' there are two broad sub-divisions: finance leases and operating leases. The definitions used by the Equipment Leasing Association[2] best explain their operational significance:

A *finance lease* is a contract involving payment over an obligatory period (the primary period) of specified sums sufficient in total to amortise the capital outlay of the lessor and give some profit. The obligatory period is less than, or at the most equal to, the estimated life of the asset. There may be a secondary period. If so, it is at the option of the lessee and the rentals are reduced in amount.

An *operating lease* is a contract where the asset is not wholly amortised during the obligatory period (if any) of the lease, and where the lessor does not rely for his profit on the rentals in the obligatory period. In some operating leases the lessor is responsible for maintenance.

The significant aspect of the lease is that the ownership and the use of the equipment are divorced. The lessee has no right to ownership in contract unless specifically provided for after the expiry of the rental period. With *hire purchase* the lessee has the option to acquire the asset for a specified or nominal sum. This option can be exercised after a given period and is, of course, conditional on the payment of due rentals. In the hire-purchase situation, ownership only passes when the option to purchase has been completed in accordance with the contract. This can be well into the working life of the equipment. Another form of transaction is the *instalment purchase*. The instalments may be akin to rental payments but possession and title pass to the user on sale.

Operational aspects

We have already seen in Chapter 4 that when a firm is considering new production plant the first main task is to shape a definite project proposal. The operational purpose and the capital cost of the new plant is established. The worth of the proposition is then assessed at the evaluation stage. If this basic worth is not confirmed, then that should be the end of the matter — irrespective of the manner of subsequent finance. If the proposal has overcome the hurdle and the manner of finance enters the authorisation dialogue, then the alternative of leasing should be evaluated. Operational, economic and financial aspects thus need to be examined separately and sequentially.

Taking first the case of a finance lease: how does it affect operational management? As we have already seen, the preparation stages of the plant investment process are just as relevant and project implementation will be the same as with company-financed projects. The user selects his own plant and this could range from a conventional, general-purpose machine to specialist equipment. He must satisfy himself as to the functional fitness and quality of the plant; there is no recourse against the lessor on this account. He normally also has to meet the costs of delivery, installation and connecting up the plant. In all operational matters he is in direct contact with the equipment supplier. Of course, no grants and allowances in respect of this equipment are due to the lessee — these accrue to the lessor, the owner of the plant. Nevertheless, one expects that such benefits are reflected in the rental.

Once the plant is ready for use, the lease requires responsible operation. This one might expect anyway, but what is taken for granted is now made explicit. The equipment is to be used in a skilful and proper manner. This requires the appropriate grade of labour, form of training and supervision. The equipment shall be kept in reasonable repair and condition and be overhauled at reasonable intervals. Such terms are general; they are the language of the contract. A plant engineer could be sceptical about their meaning, yet when it comes to litigation, with expert witnesses, these terms form an effective basis for judgement. A proper maintenance programme is required. Understandably, the lessor is entitled to inspect the equipment which cannot be removed from the specified location without his consent. Furthermore, the equipment may not be modified without his agreement and any additions or improvements accrue to him. This might be a constraint where a company is intent on continuous process development. Insurance is the responsibility of the user.

Operating leases are generally available for standard, proprietary equipment for which there is a second-hand market, such as with mobile cranes, fork lift trucks, etc. Often the lessor is the manufacturer of the equipment or an associated finance company. Apart' from a minimum contract period the leases can be for any proportion of the expected working life. This includes fixed-term contracts or indefinite periods terminable on notice. In gauging the rental level the lessor will not only consider the time scale of use but also the expected second-hand market prices. Again, maintenance and insurance will have to be paid for by the user, but where the lessor is also the manufacturer he may physically carry out overhauls. An operating lease can be matched against a particular project programme and the plant returned after its completion. The risk of redundancy or obsolescence is thus reduced.

Advantages and disadvantages of equipment leasing

It may be convenient to summarise here some of the general advantages and disadvantages of equipment leasing. They form guide lines and each company will have to assess its particular mix of pluses and minuses. Matters of taxation or contract may, of course, require professional advice.

Advantages to be secured

(i) Tax allowances and grant benefits where taxable profits are insufficient or inapplicable.

(ii) Extra *sources* of finance where otherwise liquidity problems or limited borrowing powers would be an obstacle.

(iii) An extra form of finance. It cannot be called in at short notice like an overdraft nor reduce general financial flexibility as may result from a debenture or mortgage.

(iv) The time value of money — no need to plough back into reserves to finance plant investment; ploughing and earning is simultaneous. The earlier employment of new equipment has an inflation protection component.

(v) The lease value broadly matches the investment.

(vi) The risks of equipment redundancy or obsolescence can be reduced.

Disadvantages to be considered

(i) Extra costs compared to straight ownership. Rentals include the lessor's administrative expenses and profit margin.

(ii) Alternative forms of finance, such as bank overdrafts and fixed-term loans may also be cheaper.

(iii) Finance is tied to the timing of the investment. Money rates can be high just when the plant is delivered and has to be paid for.

(iv) Payments have to be maintained, irrespective of cash flows and the state of the company's business.

Evaluating the leasing proposition

Once the operating arguments for new production equipment have been demonstrated, the expected revenue benefits need to be coupled to a finance proposition. When plant leasing is considered it can be evaluated together with other finance alternatives such as purchase or hire purchase. The lease payments are over time and a comparison with the single purchase outlay is best achieved by the DCF method, using the present value (PV) approach. What this means can be conveniently shown by a simple example.

Assume a firm needs a fork lift truck for factory use. The truck costs £10000, has a working life of four years, at the end of which it can be sold for £1000 to the second-hand market for reconditioning. The truck will show a net saving in labour costs of £12000 per annum, while its fuel, maintenance and insurance will amount to £2000 a year. The annual operational cash flow will then be £10000. The company is liable to corporation tax at 52% and estimates that, if necessary, it could borrow the money for the equipment purchase at 16%.

A proposition of this type has three forms of cash flow:

(i)   The operational cash flow
(ii)   The finance cash flow
(iii)   The tax cash flow

The operational cash flow will be the same, irrespective of the method of finance. It is essentially a function of equipment use and economics. The other two are very much affected by the choice of finance. The evaluation of different forms of finance need not take the operational cash flow into account. It is, however, helpful to do so to get an overall picture of the proposition and to see how sensitive the project outcome is to different forms of finance.

The first task is to obtain the present value (PV) of the operational cash flow. Assuming a year-end computation of net benefits at 16% we get the results shown in Table 8.1.

Table 8.1 PV of operational cash flow

End of year	Savings	Tax at 52% (a)	Cash flow	Discount factor at 16%	Present value
1	10000	—	10000	0.867	8670
2	10000	(5200)	4800	0.743	3566
3	10000	(5200)	4800	0.641	3077
4	10000	(5200)	4800	0.552	2650
5		(5200)	(5200)	0.476	(2475)
		Total present value of savings			£15488

Notes
(a)   Corporation tax is presumed payable one year later.
(b)   Cash outflows are in brackets.

The next stage is the present value calculation of the three financing alternatives.

PV of equipment purchase

This presumes a 100% tax allowance on the investment, giving a tax saving in the year following acquisition. At the end of the equipment life the plant resale proceeds give rise to a balancing charge, again lagged by one year. (See Table 8.2.)

PV of equipment lease

Assume the lease to be for four years at an annual rental of £2500 with the first payment due on agreement. The total rental payments seem to be no more than the equipment price but as the user loses all investment allowances such a rental level may not be cheap. The rentals can however be set off against taxable profits. The last payment is due at the beginning of year four which for discounting purposes is equivalent to the end of year three. Incidentally, if rentals were payable quarterly, intermediate discounting factors

Table 8.2

End of Year	Capital cash flow	Tax cash flow	Total cash flow	Discount factor at 16%	Present value
0	10 000		10 000	1.000	10 000
1		(5200)	(5200)	0.867	(4508)
2			—	0.743	—
3			—	0.641	—
4	(1000)		(1000)	0.552	(552)
5		520	520	0.476	248
	Total present value of purchase cost				£5188

Note
For the cost calculations the cash inflows are in brackets.

would be used. The principle of calculation would be the same. (See Table 8.3.)

PV of hire purchase

Consider an agreement with a 40% deposit, followed by three annual instalments of £2800 (this is equivalent to a rate of interest of just under 19%). This time the calculation is a little more complex as the user has two tax components to consider. There is the investment allowance on plant acquisition as well as the tax savings on the hire-purchase interest payments. It is therefore helpful to analyse the hire-purchase cash flow first and then compute the tax allowance on interest payment. (See Table 8.4.)

The present value calculation will then look like Table 8.5.

Summarising the overall situation, we get the following net present values for the equipment proposal at 16%.

Operating Savings £15488 + Purchase Cost (£5188) = £10300
Operating Savings £15488 + Lease Cost   (£4483) = £11005
Operating Savings £15488 + H.P. Cost   (£4652) = £10836

Table 8.3

End of Year	Lease cash flow	Tax cash flow	Total cash flow	Discount factor at 16%	Present value
0	2500		2500	1.000	2500
1	2500	(1300)	1200	0.867	1040
2	2500	(1300)	1200	0.743	892
3	2500	(1300)	1200	0.641	769
4	—	(1300)	(1300)	0.552	(718)
	Total present value of lease cost				£4483

In this example the present value of the lease alternative represents the lowest finance cost and, with the given operating savings, the highest equipment proposition value. The purpose of this illustration is to demonstrate the manner of calculation, not to show the advantage of a particular form of finance — that would depend on actual commercial terms. The illustration does however emphasise the time value of receipts and the effect of taxation. It is also interesting that the differences in finance costs are relatively greater than the differences in final project values. The richer the project yield, the less crucial become the variations in finance costs and other, non-quantitative factors may get more attention. Incidentally, with such varying finance cash flow patterns, discounting at other rates could alter the preference order of the alternatives.

Leasing and inflation

The pervasive nature of inflation has already prompted us to consider its implications when we dealt with project evaluation. The same basic arguments apply and it is particularly necessary to look at inflation aspects where the

Table 8.4 Analysis of hire-purchase cash flow

End of year	Cash flow	Outstanding debt	Interest	Debt repayment
0	4000	10 000	—	4000
1	2800	6 000	1135	1665
2	2800	4 335	820	1980
3	2800	2 355	445	2355

Table 8.5

End of Year	H.P. cash flow	Plant tax allowance	H.P. interest (a)	Tax allowance	Total cash flow	Discount factor at 16%	Present value
0	4000				4000	1.000	4000
1	2800	(5200)	1135		(2400)	0.867	(2080)
2	2800		820	(590)	2210	0.743	1642
3	2800		445	(426)	2374	0.641	1522
4	(1000)			(231)	(1231)	0.552	(680)
5		520			520	0.476	248
			Total present value of H.P. cost				£4652

Note
(a) This is part of the instalment payment.

lease is over a long period. For instance, after five years of inflation at 10% p.a. the monetary cost of a machine tool available now at £10000 will be about £16000. At the same inflation rate a lease rental payment of £1000 in five years' time will have a value of £621 in today's currency. This is quite apart from time value, discounting considerations.

Other things equal, there is a strong incentive to use equipment now and to string out rental payments as far as possible into the future. Of course, the lessor will not share such enthusiasm when he gets repaid in depreciated currency and he may well insist on renegotiation clauses on interest rates in periods of strong inflation.

If inflation is brought into the reckoning then it should enter the comparative analysis of the different finance routes. For instance, with a good second-hand plant market the resale value of equipment has an element of inflation hedge. As we have already seen in Chapter 6 inflation is difficult to forecast. Nevertheless, an evaluation of finance alternatives with different inflation assumptions will yield a number of scenarios helpful to the decision process.

References

1. Sykes, A., *The Lease-Buy Decision,* British Institute of Management, (London, 1976)
2. Equipment Leasing Association, *Equipment Leasing,* (London, 1976)

Additional reading

Aydon, C., *Financing Company Plant and Equipment,* InComTec, (London, 1974)
Vancil, R.F., *Leasing of Industrial Equipment,* McGraw-Hill, (London, 1963)

9 Life-cycle costing

When we discussed project evaluation in Chapter five we compared prospective revenue benefits with proposed capital expenditures. The benefits to be considered are incremental (typically, savings), and usually they are the net balance of gains and losses. Compared to existing plant a new unit may have certain higher costs, such as plant maintenance or insurance, as well as lower expenses, such as a reduced labour content per unit output. The category of gain must sufficiently outweigh the sum of extra costs to justify the project.

The analysis of costs and benefits is part of the project preparation task. A good analysis is not confined to one approach. Often there are a number of technical solutions to a production problem. However, their economics can be very different. To relate the technical and economic aspects of an operational task is, of course, one of the jobs of a production engineer. Take the relatively simple task of making a wheel for a toy train. First of all, the wheel could be made from different materials — this will already very much affect the type of equipment to be used. Assume a metal wheel; it could be die cast, sintered, formed, pressed, machined from bar stock, etc. Our decision making is much easier if one particular method is so promising (some hard data first, please) that we can forget the alternatives. If pressing the wheel from strip has such promise then all we need to do is to choose a suitable press. Our operational requirements are defined and we obtain plant quotations from reputable suppliers. All submissions are suitable for the application; the press with the lowest price wins and its purchase is incorporated in a project submission. Fine, but as far as life-cycle costing is concerned, this is not good enough.

The meaning of life-cycle costing

The life cycle of a production unit is the period during which it receives resources. Often this starts long before physical existence. If the unit is an in-house development the resources authorisation stage for project preparation is the moment of birth. With a purchased item it begins with the drafting of the first specification — organisational resources are being used. Birth heralds a sequence of phases: design and development, construction or acquisition, installation, commissioning, operation, maintenance and disposal. All these phases have their costs. Life-cycle costing is concerned with the totality of these costs, not just the costs of a particular stage — however important or well documented that might be.

One purpose of costing is to assist management in the effective operation of a business. Cost data is the first step towards the containment, if not the minimisation, of life-cycle costs. This is carried out in a given context which reflects the environment and the objectives of the business, e.g. defined product quality or manufacturing standards. Because of the diversity and the interactive effects of the cost constituents, the reduction of life-cycle costs is a composite activity. This activity is known as *terotechnology*. The term 'terotechnology' is based on the Greek word *tereo* which means to guard, to look after. Essentially terotechnology is about the proper management of physical assets. It has been defined as follows by the Committee for Terotechnology, Department of Industry[1]:

'Terotechnology is a combination of management, financial, engineering and other practices applied to physical assets in pursuit of economic life cycle costs. Its practice is concerned with the specification and design for reliability and maintainability of plant, machinery, equipment, buildings and structures, with their installation, commissioning, maintenance, modification and replacement, and with feedback of information on design, performance and costs'.

The important point to note is that terotechnology is inter-disciplinary — a number of specialists have to contribute to its successful application. It is not a technique in itself; rather it uses techniques, such as DCF, sensitivity analysis, risk analysis, etc. These are the techniques of quantification which form an important part of the approach. Terotechnology is a concept which takes a total, integrated view of the economic life of production plant. It is more than 'common sense', not only because of the techniques which it applies, but also because of the focus it provides for dealing with complex situations.

The basic life-cycle cost categories

Although there are as many cost constituents as there are stages in plant life, it is convenient to group them into the following four major cost categories:

1. *Capital Costs.* Essentially, these are those costs incurred on a new plant until it is ready for its specified task. Many of the initial design and engineering costs appear here in a capitalised form.
2. *Operating Costs.* These are the costs of using the plant.
3. *Support Costs.* These are all those expenses, particularly maintenance, which are needed to sustain the plant in its defined role.
4. *Disposal Costs.* These are the terminal costs of removing the plant and making good.

The minimisation of one of these cost categories may not mean minimum overall cost. The benefit of terotechnology is the difference between the optimal total cost of the plant as compared to the sum of its constituents. This reflects its role of overall optimisation, not partial trade-offs.

The scope for terotechnology

There are cases where expensive plant has been bought and its operation and maintenance have proved so costly that it now stands unused. Had terotechnology been part of the original analysis this might have been avoided. The more capital intensive a production process, the more is production hostage to physical assets, their proper use and maintenance.

A particular opportunity exists for terotechnology where there is a long plant life and the cumulative operating and support costs are large compared to the initial outlay. Here, the sins of omission at the project preparation stage may have a long and expensive life-cycle. Even with a limited plant life, terotechnology has scope where the revenue costs of plant use are heavy. Where high reliability and operational readiness levels are the basis of effective operation then support costs can escalate. This has been the case with defence systems and explains why life-cycle costing found its first applications here. Such systems are complex, sensitive, sophisticated and expensive. Furthermore they often have to operate in a political setting where capital votes are intermittent and during the long intervals there is pressure to reduce operating budgets. This makes the achievement of economic life-cycle costs a major objective.

The application of life-cycle costing

As a tool of analysis and decision making, life-cycle costing has its first opportunity at the design and process evaluation stages. Its use is illustrated by Figure 9.1.

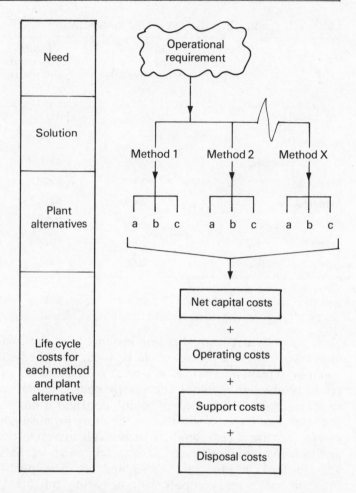

Figure 9.1 The role of life-cycle costing in equipment selection

An operational requirement has to be met — say, we want to make 100000 toy train wheels a week at a target cost of 5p each. As we have already seen, our solutions to this need are a number of different production methods. Each of these methods can be linked with a number of plant alternatives.

Table 9.1   Simplified life-cycle cost computation

	Method 1 Press work plant alternative (a)	Method 2 Die casting plant alternative (a)	(b)
Net capital cost (£)	16000	24000	35000
Annual costs			
Production labour	9000	4000	2000
Materials	2000	3000	3000
Maintenance	2000	1000	3000
Plant services	1000	2000	2000
Tooling	2000	1000	1000
Down time losses	2000	4000	1000
Total annual operating and support costs	£18000	£15000	£12000

New plant is to be bought. For instance, for presswork a number of different presses could be used; thus method one could have plant alternatives a, b or c. With a number of different production methods and several plant alternatives for each method, the choice of plant configurations could become quite large. A shortlist of the more promising alternatives can then be submitted to the full life-cycle costing analysis. As an illustration of our approach let us have another look at our train wheel and see how presswork (method one) would compare with die casting (method two). We find that we could install a press with related equipment (alternative 1a) for a total cost of £16000. With die casting we have a choice; we can install a standard unit for £24000 (alternative 2a) or a semi-automatic machine for £35000 (alternative 2b). For the extra capital expenditure we get a reduction in labour costs and a more reliable unit. However, the equipment is more sophisticated and this will entail higher maintenance charges. Table 9.1 summarises the

Table 9.2 Discounted life-cycle costs for three plant alternatives

Costs	Year	Plant alternatives		
		1a	2a	2b
Net capital cost	0	16000	24000	35000
Annual operating and support costs discounted at 16%	1 to 5	60344	50288	40230
Life-cycle cost		£76344	74288	75230

various operating and support expenses for a five-year life-cycle. To simplify the problem we have neglected inflation, learning curve effects, plant disposal values and other variables that may apply in practice. On this basis Table 9.2 shows the life-cycle costs of the alternatives. These costs are not just a summation of cash flows. The time value of money matters, and here we have assumed that the company expects a 16% return on its investments.

It will be seen that the sum of capital and discounted operating/support costs gives the standard die casting unit (method 2a) the advantage. Note that the revenue costs, although reduced by discounting, are more than the capital costs. This applies to most manufacturing situations. The disparity would be greater still with a longer plant life.

There are two main benefits from this type of computation. The first is in the costing task itself. To put costs to such items as downtime or maintenance requires their detailed scrutiny in the first place. The very examination of figures has its surprises and lessons. Quick estimates without data will not do. We therefore need an information system which gives us the raw material for proper analysis. In turn, such a system needs to be planned so that the data for decisions comes naturally and economically. The upheavals of special investigations are not always matched by the quality of the obtained data.

Furthermore, our quest for systematic information about prospective production plant will bear on the relationships with equipment suppliers. What matters to a customer cannot be entirely ignored. Further information may be made available about key performance factors or other user experience may be harnessed.

The second main benefit is with the analysis of the life-cycle costs. The implications of and the alternatives to the tabled costs can be considered.

Trade-off evaluation

Tables 9.1 and 9.2 have furnished a basic set of alternatives. They are not the end of the matter, but rather a set of benchmarks. We have now a scale for life-cycle costs. The bigger the revenue costs component, the greater is the case for a detailed review of the marshalled data. We are looking for trade-offs — possible changes in cost patterns. How much can we reduce operating and support costs? What changes and plant modifications would this involve? How much would that cost? With discounted cash flow the extra, immediate capital expenditure can be related to future savings in operating costs. The dialogue is not only in-house but also with suppliers. Nor is it confined to capital/revenue alternatives. Any change in mix should be considered if it suggests a cost reduction.

Acquisition costs — maintenance costs

A detailed maintenance evaluation of the proposed equipment is necessary. Often maintenance costs can be reduced without increased capital costs if details are picked up in time. This occurs where some features of the new equipment can be to customer choice, such as the detailed location of access panels, test connections, etc. This often reduces the labour content of inspection and testing. Where a new unit will be purpose-built, maintenance trade-offs should be part of the design study. The holding of maintenance spares should also be analysed. For instance, with a large shell and tube heat exchanger the tubes are often made in batches to suit the exchanger assembly requirements. The marginal cost of an extra 5% in the tube quantity is modest and this is generally reflected in the main order price. The same 5% ordered subsequently as spares could become very expensive because of the set-up costs of a small run of 'specials'.

When the scale of operation is substantial the standardisation of maintenance facilities and equipment can have important economies of scale. Similarly, the maintenance manpower spectrum needs to be considered. Is there a need for contract maintenance or can it be done in-house?

Acquisition costs — reliability

To a plant engineer reliability is an important but mainly implicit aspect. He often has his own inbuilt 'distrust factor' for new plant proposals. The benefits of his intuitive judgement can be supplemented by a measure of quantification. How often is the plant likely to break down and for what reasons? What will be the cost of component replacement and what will be the losses due to the required plant shutdown? What extra features can be incorporated to improve reliability? Can standby units be brought in automatically on plant failure? Can automatic plant be manually operated in a crisis? What monitoring devices would assist diagnosis and provide early warning? What is the frequency and content of preventive maintenance? The answer to such questions involves the assessment of risks, costs and benefits.

Acquisition costs — expected plant life

We have already seen that the expected plant life is a function of operating inferiority which includes both deterioration, and obsolescence. Our main concern here is with the rate of physical deterioration, such as wear or fatigue, which sets a limit to useful plant life. This is reached when plant support costs become unacceptable or there is a sudden, irremediable plant failure. In the process industries corrosion is often a predictable form of deterioration. For instance, an increase of 5mm in the shell thickness of a reactor vessel could extend its operational life by two years. Alternatively, we could line the inside and get another five years from the unit. We have a trade-off between increases in capital costs and the discounted future benefits of extended plant life. Such an evaluation is best at the plant specification or design stage and reminds us of its relevance to life-cycle costing.

Acquisition costs — plant service costs

Plant services mainly consist of compressed air, cooling water, refrigerants, electricity and all forms of fuel. In terms of costs these services can be anything from a minor component to a major charge, such as electric power for the manufacture of aluminium or fuel costs for a glass furnace. For convenience, effluents can also be taken under this heading. The costs and problems of their disposal have risen substantially in recent years and will increase further with legislation to preserve the environment. There are trade-offs between different services, such as steam and electricity for process heating. There are also trade-offs with a given service such as the choice between the recycling and the discharge of cooling water. Even the time pattern of service use is important where, for instance, differential tariffs are charged for electricity, or where demand peaks invoke a penal rate. In all such cases there are capital costs, utility consumption costs and maintenance cost components to be integrated within life-cycle costs.

Future energy cost trends are, of course, important and sensitivity analysis can assist trade-off decisions. For instance, a differential cost trend of 5%, 10%, 15% or 20% between natural gas and fuel-oil prices can be related to the design specification of an industrial baking/drying oven. When would the extra costs of dual firing systems be justified? When should there be a complete switch from one fuel source to the other? What tariff negotiation objectives should be set? Again, life-cycle costing is available as a tool for decision making and bargaining.

The role of terotechnology

As we have seen, terotechnology is concerned with the cost effectiveness of production plant over the whole of its expected life span. Generally speaking, cost effectiveness analysis presumes the operational case for a particular proposition, which might have an economic justification, but need not; it could have social welfare or military objectives. Life-cycle costing is therefore an overall approach to cost effectiveness analysis.

Life-cycle costing is related to investment evaluation but differs from it. The benefit computation in terms of increased contribution (cost reduction or expansion) is excluded. It is more concerned with the content of the investment proposition than the case for the investment in the first place.

Terotechnology emphasises effective project preparation. This has often been the underestimated part of the investment process. Its wider use will therefore be a contribution to better plant investments and, hopefully, to better returns on capital.

The introduction of terotechnology will require a more rigorous level of management. A quantitative approach needs a data base. Without it, life-cycle costing cannot be applied. It is not only needed for investigation, planning and decision making; it is subsequently required for feedback and control. Life-cycle costing on an *ad hoc* basis is unlikely to achieve much. Where plant investments are an ongoing part of corporate strategy, operating and reporting systems need to fit that intent.

Two particular communication problems need to be solved for the successful application of terotechnology. The first is between the evaluating accountant, the project sponsor (whoever he is in line management) and the plant engineer. Costs of plant maintenance are often underrated. A plant quotation and specification look definitive; support cost consequences are not always fully appreciated and often mentally discounted. Such implications need to be worked through systematically with plant engineers before the project proposal is finalised.

The second main communication problem is between plant users and suppliers. In some industries their fortunes are so strongly linked that close cooperation is well established. In other cases commercial aspects and the bother of data collection have militated against it. However, the achievement of economic life-cycle costs is valuable to the supplier, as much of the plant replacement demand is affected by operating experience. Complaints, warranty claims, spares demand, service or contract maintenance reports are important indicators for equipment improvement programmes. The output of the supplier, the asset of the user, successful and economic production plant is a good contribution to their joint prosperity.

Check list: Life cycle costing

NOTE: The check lists for project preparation and plant replacement should also be used here.

1. Who prepares the specifications for new production plant?
2. What feedback on design, performance and costs are available to him?
3. Who is consulted when the specifications are drawn up?
4. What evaluation techniques are used?

5. What cost projections are made?
6. Are the present values of life-cycle costs obtained?
7. How are plant attributes listed and compared? How are such data recorded, stored and retrieved?
8. What trade-off evaluations are undertaken?
9. What discussions take place with suppliers to reduce life-cycle costs?
10. What information is fed back to them on plant performance and suggested improvements?
11. Are design and development costs identified for new plant?
12. Are plant commissioning costs determined and recorded for future guidance?
13. Are maintenance and downtime costs systematically recorded and available?
14. Are claims and assumptions about reliability and maintainability questioned and confirmed?

Reference

1. Committee for Terotechnology, Department of Industry, *Life Cycle Costing in the Management of Assets,* HMSO, (London, 1977)

Additional reading

Blanchard, B.S., *Design and Manage to Life Cycle Costs,* M/A Press, (Portland, Oregon, 1978)
Committee for Terotechnology, Department of Industry, HMSO, (London, 1975):
 (i) *Life Cycle Costing*

(ii) *An Introduction to the Management of Physical Resources*

Harvey, G., *Life Cycle Costing: A Review of the Technique,* Management Accounting, (London, October 1976)

Thackara, A.D., *Terotechnology — What it is all about,* The Chartered Mechanical Engineer, (London, June 1975)

10 Project presentation and authorisation

The brief is ready! The project is defined, documented, justified and evaluated; often it has travelled far. It has survived doubts, conflicts, the tugs of organisational war — now it waits in the ante-room of the decision makers. An interesting account of the behavioural aspects of project presentation is given by Hopwood[1].

This chapter is primarily concerned with how it makes its entry and what happens on arrival. We are interested in the presentation process so far as this reflects administrative practice within the total investment system. Similarly, we wish to look at some aspects of the decision process, known as project authorisation. In analysis the two processes are, of course, quite distinct; in practice they can be very close.

Project presentation

The reader will recall that in Figure 4.3 'The structure of project preparation' the overall investment system included the specific decision to present the proposal for authorisation. It might have seemed self-evident for the project sponsors to have taken their chance and automatically submitted their proposal in the belief that it was for top management to make the final decision. A project might look marginal or worse in a quantitative sense, yet have other arguments in its favour. Not only is it a matter here of delegating upwards, but the information environment at board level might provide better overall judgement. Indeed, the proposal itself has an information function, quite apart from the decision aspects. It can be a form of reporting or briefing on issues close to the interests of top management — we have then, in essence, the 'pro-forma' proposal. On the other hand, if a case lacked real merit, the sponsor's reputation would be at risk, although one could have expected such projects to have been filtered out at an earlier stage. Much, of course, depends here on the relationship between the decision makers and the project patrons.

There are cases where the authorisation process is in part anticipated by the presentation decision. A board may instruct its management or evaluating accountants not to present projects which are to be justified on economic grounds unless the yield is, say, 15%. In that respect the presentation decision becomes a specific type of filter.

The mechanics of presentation

A further look at the mechanics of presentation is justified here. What, in the first instance, is meant by presentation and who makes it? Are there defined routes and do these vary with the size or source of the proposal? Presentation here means the formulated request for capital resources by someone entitled to ask for them and addressed to those who can authorise them. Depending on the project value, presentation therefore will be from the organisational level immediately below the authorisation level, e.g. from the production manager to the factory manager, or from the managing director to his board. A project can thus climb several levels of the organisational hierarchy before being presented. It could fall at such intervening levels if support were withheld, yet it could not be authorised then. This is the process of endorsement, not authorisation.

Three of the four companies studied in detail defined the presentation routes in their instruction manuals. Thus, company A required all submissions to be made by a certain level of manager to the assistant managing director. In a similar vein, company C specified submission, in the first instance, to the group production director of all factory projects over £1000. The functional project source affected its route. So did size. The route was shorter for smaller projects where the amounts were within the discretion of intermediate levels of management. The route was frequently defined by the format of the capital expenditure application form.

The formal route was thus defined; the speed along it was hostage to other considerations. Much depends on the attitude of certain members of the authorisation group, typically, the full-time director within whose functional area of control the project proposal was developed. If he was personally identified with the project and keen to see it to fruition he was likely to assist with the presentation task.

Apart from the presentation route, procedures generally were defined in some detail. In companies B, C and D it was the task of management accountants to ensure that procedures were followed. With the last two companies, instructions were specific and detailed, such as the obtaining of signatures, verification of form completeness, the issue of reference numbers, entry on application registers, etc.

A significant part of the presentation procedure related to the timetable of submission. For all projects of substance the timetable of submission was governed by the calendar of board meetings. For instance, with company D all projects to be considered by the board had to be received by the group management accountant at least ten days before the appropriate meeting. Of course, some very large projects might warrant special meetings. But apart from these, the flow of project proposals had a certain unevenness with minor peaks of project presentation when sponsors were anxious to catch a particular board meeting. The beginning of the annual budget period was particularly busy as projects were brought forward for sanction. Minor items such as office furniture were generally submitted at regular intervals, say quarterly, for collective authorisation.

All but a few projects were submitted in accordance with the specified procedures. Special situations did at times arise and in such cases the system was short circuited. This occurred with plant emergencies (although that was also covered by procedures in company C) and special commercial situations — such as the obtaining of significant concessions or discounts on immediate plant orders. In these cases the decisions were confirmed by subsequent systems actuation. The commercial opportunities were more in the nature of timing than content; the intent had largely been formulated when external developments clinched the matter.

The capital expenditure request document

The analysis of the capital expenditure request documents of a number of companies indicates that the precise format and content reflect company systems which in turn are a function of the company's business. For instance, tooling costs are sufficiently frequent in the engineering industry to be a printed heading with some companies. A food company gives similar attention to ingredient savings. The design of appropriate forms is therefore a bespoke business. Documents have to reflect the needs of decision makers — this is basic to the design of any information and decision system. Nevertheless, the capital investment decision process has a set of principles which are independent of context and these must be acknowledged in detailed form design. While there is no ideal form which fits every company it is still possible to list the basic features of a good set of documents.

This section is concerned with the core of the submission document. The reader can relate his company situation to this core and add such other material as may be necessary. It is appreciated that small, routine projects would not need extensive documentation. Companies often have different documents for projects above or below specified values. For small projects the questioning on the form is simplified but there is no different of principle.

The capital project document

Form design

The two main considerations here are:

 (i) the mechanics of form filling;
(ii) the process of information assimilation and decision
      making.

Form design was originally part of organisation and methods work (O & M) but has increasingly become the task of the systems analyst. This development is mainly due to two factors. The first is the growing use of computer-based systems. 'Why not let the computer do the form filling as well as the calculations?' The second is the role of the project form(s) for related purposes, such as project cash control or management information summaries.

The main features to be considered are:

1. The size and shape of forms.
2. The number of copies, their colour and distribution.
3. The title and the reference number of the form.
4. The numbering of forms or projects.
5. The pre-printing of standard or recurring items.
6. The structuring of the form layout to correspond to the
   logic of analysis.
7. Subsequent binding or filing.

The main operational constituents

1. The title and reference number of the project.
2. A brief description of the purpose, scope and operational
   gains from the project.

3. A project expenditure summary comprising fixed assets, working capital and revenue expenses.
4. Project capital receipts: expected grants and realisations.
5. Project tax allowances.
6. Net project capital cost.
7. Capital expenditure cash flow distribution.
8. Project location: division, factory.
9. Asset categories: land, buildings, plant and machinery, vehicles, etc.
10. Value of redundant/replaced plant.
11. Project starting and expected completion dates.
12. Expected plant life.
13. Justification category: expansion, cost reduction, etc.
14. Evaluation horizon, years.
15. Cash flow due to project, per annum, average.
16. Method of computation: DCF, return on investment, payback.
17. Depreciation: method, rate, amounts.
18. Depreciation tax allowances.
19. After tax cash flow.
20. Project return (on the basis of 16).
21. Budget reference and provision (if any).
22. Remarks. These should include the key assumptions made and the implications if the project does not go forward.

Administrative and control requirements
1. Manager submitting the document: role, signature, date.
2. Originator of document.
3. Specialists responsible for aspects of the project proposal.
4. Project evaluators.
5. Endorsement signatures, depending on route of presentation.
6. Authorisation level.
7. Decision: nature, date, signature.

Supporting schedules

1. Description of buildings, plant and processes.
2. Outline site, buildings or plant layout.
3. Main plant item list.
4. Specialist technical/operational evaluations and submissions: guarantees, planning consents, etc.
5. Procurement cash flow pattern and capital expenditure graph.
6. Project benefit: analysis and cash flow explanation.
7. Project design, engineering and management charges.
8. Project organisation.
9. Contingencies and provisions.

The list indicates the core operational inputs to the plant investment decision. There are further important specialist inputs in some industries. For instance, in the manufacture of chemical intermediates a forward contract to cover the plant output could be the most important document. What has been listed is the raw material for structured project presentation from operational levels. Specialist legal, financial, foreign exchange, taxation or other professional advice may also have to be sought for important projects. But usually the point of departure for this is a well-prepared operational proposition in the first place.

Other documents

Emergency request forms. These are used if an emergency requires immediate action and the formal authorisation system needs to be short circuited. An emergency may arise from an accident or a major production breakdown. The document records the on-the-spot decision and verbal authorisation. It requires a statement of the emergency situation, the proposed course of action, its estimated costs and the authorised commitment level.

Supplementary requests. When the project costs are likely to exceed the authorised amount a supplementary authorisation/review system is usually actuated in respect of the additional expenditure. The form which gives expression to it requires an explanation of the situation, an enumeration and justification of the changes involved or an account of the extra costs where the project remains unchanged. The administrative and control requirements of the original project submission are repeated and wherever possible authorisation should be at one level higher than the previous decision.

The character of the authorisation group

It is relevant to the study of the authorisation process to look at the decision makers in their organisational setting. It is commonplace to designate such people as 'top management', but this umbrella term hides a number of relationships. Perhaps the most useful way to show these is by actual examples.

In all cases the ultimate authority and responsibility for authorisation rested with the main board of directors of the company or group of companies concerned. Such authority can be divided into two categories:

1. Direct authority. This concerns the definition of the capital expenditure system and associated policies. It also refers to the actual decision making about projects as defined within the system (these are the projects above a stated minimum of size or import).
2. Delegated authority. This covers the decision making of groups or individuals subordinate to the main board, whose authority to make investment decisions could be instituted, varied or cancelled by the main board.

Case example A

Since a merger in 1964 company A formed a division within a larger group. Ultimate authority rested with the board of the holding company. However, the relationships between company A and its parent reflected a large measure of decentralisation. Company A became a public company in 1935 and had acquired a position of prominence in its field. The development of its name, goodwill and general reputation was unaffected by the 1964 merger.

One of the reasons for this merger was the company's need to have stronger financial support for its expansion plans. The holding company provided and controlled this support. The group policy board, consisting of the group chairman, managing director, finance director and one non-executive director, made the major decisions. No directors from company A were on this committee.

Overall appropriations for capital expenditure were made on an annual basis but this did not prevent company A from making application for a specified project authorisation at any time. 75% of the company's annual depreciation cash flow could be applied within the discretion of the company; the remainder could be allotted by the group managing director as he thought appropriate.

It was interesting to note, as an example of the initiative afforded by decentralisation that the capital evaluation manual developed by company A was adopted by the whole of the group.

Case example B

The history and the development of company B was different in character from company A. Its operation was more centralised and although the division, whose capital projects were investigated, was the major operating unit of the company in terms of turnover and profit, it had traded for many years under the company's name — in a sense, it generated the company image to the outside world. The executive director responsible for this, and an allied division, was on the main board of the company and its executive committee. This committee consisted of eight executive directors who met monthly with the managing director as chairman. The committee was responsible for running the day-to-day routine of the business of the company. Minutes of its meeting were discussed by the main board. Capital expenditure applications for projects up to £100000 were dealt with by the finance committee. Larger project applications had to be considered by the main board.

Case example C

This company broadly doubled in size (assets, turnover, labour employed) during the period 1965-70. Much of this growth was due to a policy of acquisition. The company had developed a formal group structure and this account refers to its main subsidiary. The distinction between this subsidiary and the holding company was relatively fine, for the subsidiary was the original and the main operating unit of the group. Its chairman was the chairman of the holding company and its managing director was also on the main board. Three of the five main board members were on the board of the subsidiary. Despite its substantial size the company still had strong family associations and traditions and this was reflected in the board compositions. The two boards made the main investment decisions but their interlocking nature suggested that the same people were primarily involved.

Case example D

The main decision group on capital investments was the board of the holding company, several members of which were formerly associated with the constituent businesses which merged in 1948 to form company D.

Comment

Some interesting points emerge from these case illustrations. Firstly, most of the decision makers seem to have been full-time executives and as such were familiar with the operational context. Secondly, there was a tendency towards specialisation at board level as far as the detailed scrutiny of proposals was concerned. Thirdly, more than one board might be involved with authorisation, although effective power tended to be with one group of decision makers.

The delegated authorisation of capital expenditure

It was already noted in Chapter 2 that hundreds of projects might be authorised by a company of substance during its financial year. In most cases, the frequency and respective values of these projects conform broadly to a Pareto distribution, with the bulk of the projects being of small value and representing simple plant acquisitions. A standard practice relating to the delegated authorisation of minor capital expenditure is common in such circumstances. One can further observe a partial correlation between the level of authority within the hierarchy and the amounts which can be authorised. Limits are set on individual amounts as well as on cumulative or time rate expenditures. A typical pattern of delegation is shown on Table 10.1.

Such a tabulation can only be indicative. Overall company levels of capital expenditure vary considerably, not only because of the scale of operation, but also with the capital intensity of production processes. Furthermore, titles do not adequately indicate the standing of a particular organisational role within the overall structure. The object of a delegation system is to process the many small projects which in value constitute only a modest proportion of the total capital expenditure. Many routine projects reflect a given machine value category. Where technological factors are a significant determinant of project values this is often reflected by the authorisation framework. For instance, company B which operated standard production lines had many projects around the £10000 mark which usually involved a standard module for such a line. Divisional authorisation levels matched this project value. Different limits were often speci-

fied for various project categories. In one case there was no
delegated authority for expansion projects; only for replacement and modernisation. Another important factor affecting
discretion levels was whether or not the project was included
in the capital expenditure budget.

Cumulative project authorisation limits were generally set
by the annual capital expenditure budgets, broken down pro-
portionately for each level of management. In a number of
cases the permitted annual total seemed to be about five times
the maximum individual project value.

On the whole, the extent of financial delegation below
director level is relatively limited. While certain scope may be
given to divisional boards, control at factory manager level
tends to be tight. In larger companies the level of divisional
discretion reflects performance in terms of return on capital
employed. The time-lag effect of continuous inflation tends
to erode the real worth of managerial autonomy despite the
periodic increase of discretion limits.

The administrative practice of authorisation

Major projects are authorised at board meetings and the
minutes of the meeting are the evidence of authorisation. In
some cases there is a further signature by the chairman or
managing director on the formal project document with or
without reference to the board minute concerned. Where
authorisation is delegated, the signature of the appropriate
executive is usually sufficient.

In administrative terms authorisation sets off a number of
tasks, such as formal notification of approval to the project
applicants, the accounts and purchasing departments, the
issue of job and accounts numbers, etc.

The authorisation process is not confined to mere yes/no
decisions. For instance, a rejection could be combined with
the request for one or several subsequent alternative submissions. Projects could be scaled down where a number of

Table 10.1 Some patterns of project authorisation limits

Level ↓	Pattern → A £	B £	C — Item in budget £	C — Item not in budget
Factory manager Factory director	2 500	2 000	2 000	250
Divisional director Divisional managing director	5 000	5 000	40 000	10 000
Divisional committee (below board level)	25 000	—	—	—
Company managing director (or deputy M.D.)	—	10 000	—	—
Group managing director or deputy	—	—	100 000	100 000
Board finance committee	—	250 000	—	—

identical plant items were required. Where sequential cost commitments are involved the first stages could be approved and the remainder rejected or, more likely, deferred. Alternatively, the whole project could be postponed or deferred to a later board meeting, often with requests for additional information.

Authorisation does not always give automatic sanction to incur expenditure. Whilst with the more limited setting of the factory manager's financial discretion there is little point in delaying the authorised expenditure, the larger sums, greater complexity or uncertainty of the situation at main board level prompts some boards to apply finer controls of cash releases. Thus a 'tap' system of detail sanction within the global authorisation might be used by the board or an executive director for internal or external expenditure. Where the project engineering and design content is considerable the board may permit internal expenditure on such work, yet stop all external commitments. Often this is done to retain technologists who might in the short run be underemployed or redundant.

It is a form of limited risk taking. The cost of such work is carried forward as part of the total project capital expense, or written off if in the end the project is abandoned.

In some instances there is also a time-lag in the operation of the tap system. The board formally accepts the commitment of the investment proposal but regards cash expenditure release as a separate decision problem.

In addition to the board's control of capital expenditure, administrative expenditure release systems could provide a further mechanism of authorisation and control. The practice of company C provides a good example. In support of project applications it was necessary to specify the required plant items and their costs in some detail. Estimates were also submitted in respect of plant accessories, transport charges and installation costs. Similarly, building and engineering services costs were also to be tabled in an itemised form. Project authorisation included approval of the project scheme and plant item list. Subsequently, expenditure requisitions arising from the project had to be forwarded to the assistant group chief accountant for verification that the requisitions were in line with the proposed project scheme. Only then would commitments be authorised. The example also suggests that there is no precise boundary between authorisation as such and subsequent project financial control.

Supplementary authorisation

Where a project proposal has been sanctioned to the amount requested, the permission to spend further monies on the project is usually given by supplementary authorisations. Such additional sanction may be due to a variety of reasons. In most cases the extra expenditure is unattractive to the authorisation group. Quite apart from the administrative bother, it suggests that the proposal met with complications in implementation and that certain predictions were mistaken. More seriously, the economics of the project may be affected; the investment looks correspondingly less attractive.

The main causes of additional expense are as follows:

General inflation effects during the project duration. This is primarily seen in terms of higher labour costs and equipment charges. The increase in expense is a function of the project period.

Equipment and design changes. These are part of the process of full plant definition which may not be complete at the proposal stage. There could still be unresolved technical problems, the solutions of which turn out to be more expensive than first anticipated.

Project implementation difficulties. These are unexpected troubles which arise during the project execution. For instance, in factory construction an unprecedented storm causes a landslide and requires extensive remedial work.

Project delays. Where the project schedule is exceeded and manpower resources need to be employed for longer than budgeted, then excess costs have to be absorbed.

Improvements. Two source categories can be established here. Where a project has an extended planning stage, particularly when linked with engineering/development work, there is the opportunity to incorporate improved versions of the plant or processes into the project. Extra costs are normally associated with these, not only because of the further call on resources but also due to the possible disturbance effects of their introduction into an ongoing project. The other source of improvement is within the project itself. It arises from the detailed definition work which is part of the project implementation. In that sense it is related to *Equipment and design changes* (above).

Extra expenses due to improvement are more acceptable and controllable than the other types. Nevertheless, there is the dilemma of choice between the benefits of effective project execution and the yield from the latest knowledge. If the improvement content is substantial it could lead to a major project reconstruction, or to a separate project.

Administrative provision for excess expenditures

The authorisation procedures for supplementary project expenditures can be divided into two distinct categories. The first is that of implicit authorisation. The authorisation group accepts the limits of estimate accuracy and the hazards of project implementation; it establishes an expenditure tolerance for minor overruns without re-actuating the whole submission and authorisation mechanism. The tightness of such tolerances is, of course, a matter of judgement and experience. For instance, company A specified ±5% of the approved figure, company C permitted an excess of 10%, company D an excess of £1000 or 5%, whichever greater, of the capital value in respect of an existing project authorisation. (These are non-inflation tolerances; separate provision would be required for inflation effects.) Excess expenditure within the given limits did not reduce responsibility, but contained administrative work.

Where the amounts in question exceed the set limits, explicit authorisation is required and a supplementary capital expenditure request system is activated. Such a system is usually designed to focus attention on the reasons for excess expenditure. In the excess expenditure situation one can isolate changes in project scope from other causes of over-expenditure. Such alterations in scope were reflected in the system of company C which required the notification to the assistant group chief accountant together with the relevant changes in costs. Changes in project scope were recognised as causes of excess expenditure by the other company systems, although not specifically referred to in their project documentation.

While changes in scope often increased project costs, or were used as a justification for this, there were instances where a reduction in expenditure resulted. In extreme cases a project might no longer be necessary. The systems operated by companies A and C allowed for such possibilities. With company A, requests for sanction to reduce or to cancel a project were required. In default of this the project originators would be held to the undertaking of their project submission.

A particular aspect of the supplementary request procedure is associated with project cost control. In most cases the request is made in anticipation of excess costs, but authorisation can also be retrospective to formalise excess expenditure already incurred.

Check list: Project presentation

1. Have all forms been completed?
2. Is the supporting material available in submission form? Key specifications, plant lists, drawings?
3. Has all presentation liaison taken place with affected departments, particularly the accounting function?
4. Have all supporting signatures been obtained?
5. Have all code/accounting numbers been specified?
6. Have you checked the project submission category (if any)?
   a. Already in Budget.
   b. Extra to Budget.
   c. 'Emergency.
   d. Supplementary, etc.
7. At what authorisation level will the project be considered?
8. Is there a submission timetable for this authorisation level?
9. What is the distribution list for project presentation?

10. How are supplementary requests dealt with? What special scrutiny do they get?
11. What procedures are there for emergency requests and their documentary follow-up?

Reference

1. Hopwood, A., *Accounting and Human Behaviour,* Haymarket Publishing, (London, 1974)

11 Project implementation

'The project is on!' This watershed phrase, followed by the countersigned project application form or a special letter of authorisation, marks the beginning of the next stage of the investment process — the project implementation stage. For the sake of simplicity we shall assume an uncomplicated authorisation process — no conditional or part authorisation — an unqualified agreement to a direct request.

Project implementation is concerned with the realisation of the first part of the project intention, i.e. the provision of the physical facilities needed to generate the desired economic performance. This first-stage objective itself has to be achieved within set technical, operational, financial and timetable terms. The task of such achievement is often given to those who develop the project justification in the first instance — with many companies this is a matter of policy. It is thus common to see members of the project preparation group subsequently concerned with implementation. There are, of course, significant benefits of continuity with such an arrangement. The actual mix will vary with project and company; there is a division of labour, very much affected by project size, between specialist estimators and full-time project engineers.

Just as there is likely to be a carry-over of people from the preparation to the implementation stage, so there is an element of continuity in the organisational framework. This chapter is first concerned with the systems aspects of project implementation. It then considers some aspects of project control with particular reference to two major project criteria: time and cost.

The concept of project implementation

This part of the overall investment process is mainly described in textbooks on project management. Such books are couched in normative terms; they are designed to help the practitioner. It is not our intention to emulate them in detail, yet our account would be incomplete if no reference were made to the organisational and physical activities which constitute the very process of investment. The progress of authorised projects, especially those of major significance to the well-being of the firm, remains the ultimate concern of the project authorisation group. Here come the first feedback signals on the venture. The fortunes or otherwise of the implementation stage colour the judgement of the decision makers and thus influence their attitudes towards new investment proposals. Theories of investment take no account of projects already authorised by the firm but still in the implementation stage. Yet some projects may take years to implement and their prolongation, beyond the set schedule and for whatever reason, can have major cash flow implications.

A brief description of the implementation stage is therefore desirable and it is perhaps most convenient if this is expressed in systems terms. Figure 11.1 illustrates the various constituents of this part of the total investment process. The implementation stage begins with the project brief and ends with the plant handover to the operating group which will commission the completed plant. The boundary between

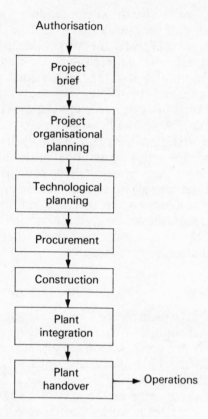

Figure 11.1 Simplified block diagram for project implementation

these two stages is not always clearly defined, but usually
project implementation represents a capital cost, whereas
commissioning costs are generally treated as an operating
expense.

The project brief

The project brief is the actuating mechanism of the
implementation stage. Its format may be a standard

document or a specific memorandum. It normally comes from the authorisation group and is addressed to the managers responsible for project implementation. The project brief can be regarded as having three distinct functions. Firstly, it is an instruction, a command, that something shall be done. Secondly, it provides such information as may be needed to clarify what has to be done. In practice, this usually means reference to the project proposal itself, which on authorisation becomes the framework for action. Additional information may be given, such as target dates or cash release programmes. Thirdly, the project brief can serve as evidence of authorisation to use company resources up to specified amounts. Depending on the nature of the project, the brief itself often reflects a dialogue between members of the authorisation group and the designated project manager.

Project organisational planning

The project which receives relatively prompt authorisation has the advantage of continuity; the project preparation group may not yet be disbanded and its members diverted to other tasks. This does not mean that they will be automatically chosen for the next stage; but very often they are. If the majority of the group are thus transferred the organisational framework is often also carried forward, at least in principle. The major difference between the preparation and implementation stages is the scale of project operation. This has organisational implications. Apart, perhaps, for the development biased project with a large technical content, most of the detailed work of implementation is understandably avoided at the preparation stage. Once a measure has been obtained of the technical risks, resources commitment at the preparation stage is conditioned by the likelihood of authorisation. There is little point in major expenditures before a decision has been made. But now, after authorisation, a project group might have to grow tenfold. The framework of operation, if not available from previous comparative projects, must be quickly established. This is the purpose of the project organisational planning stage.

The main constituents of this project planning stage are given below. Although listed here in sequence some will be developed concurrently in practice. The context of a major project will be presumed, say, one worth over £1 000 000 at 1970 prices. The same framework may hold for smaller projects, but would then be rather less formalised.

Project organisation. This is concerned with the definition of the project management role and the appointment of the project manager and his assistants. It settles the project structure, i.e. the manner in which the project is to be carried out. For instance, it decides whether the project manager is to be a line manager with specialist staff directly responsible to him or whether his task is to coordinate and progress the work of specialists answerable to their own functional managers.

Project systems definition. This is the specification of all administrative procedures relating to the project. It establishes the pattern of information flow and the manner of coordination within which specialist contributions are integrated to achieve the overall project objectives. The manner of project reporting and control in terms of time and money is particularly important here.

Project representation. We are concerned here with the formal relationships between the project group, through its management, and other interested parties. These relationships can be seen as an extension of the project systems. For instance, with top management they would be concerned with the manner of cost and progress reporting, cash flow requirements, etc. The relationship with the client department, factory or division may be expressed in detailed formal procedures. The client group is the internal organisational unit which will operate the plant furnished by the project. If it is a profit centre it will pay, internally, for the project costs. However, most of the dialogue will concentrate on technical, operational and schedule matters. The third major relationship is with contractors and plant suppliers. This can vary in range from the detailed definition of procedures with one main contractor, as is the practice in some process industries, to some general principles applicable to a wide spectrum of different contracts.

Project framework planning. It is an aspect of initiative, which is part of project management, to take the overall project objectives, as defined in the implementation brief, and to break these into meaningful sub-targets for both internal and external project contributors. In essence, these are scheduling tasks if they involve time, or budget apportionments if they relate to costs. In practice, these may be linked. Thus a section of electrical engineers, working on a chemical plant project, might be given a budget for electric motors and starters, equivalent to 8% of the overall project estimate, an engineering time budget of 1000 hours and a time scale of equipment delivery and installation which is integrated within an overall project programme. It is this type of detailed decision making, related to the planning of project execution, which is the most prevalent activity of the first phase of the project implementation stage. Much of the project success will depend on the thoroughness of this work.

Textbooks on project management have given much attention to the techniques available for this planning task. Particularly important here are network analysis techniques such as CPM (critical path method), PERT (programme evaluation review technique), PERT/COST; all of which are suitable for computer use. Line balancing and resource scheduling are other important aids for this planning stage. It is not possible to develop these techniques here and the interested reader is advised to consult the works of such writers at Moder and Phillips[1], Hajek[2] and Hackney[3]. Suffice it to say that these techniques have had a significant effect on the management of large projects and that it is one of the skills of a project manager to specify not only what techniques are to be used but also the manner and extent of their application. The techniques have their costs, of course, but the benefits from more effective project management and control more than justify these.

One general point needs to be made about some of the listed organisational planning activities. Where the scale and frequency of operation justifies it these will be pre-planned and defined as general practice for all projects over a given size, i.e. there is an organisational tooling-up which reduces the content of such activities in the typical project.

Technological planning

This stage is primarily concerned with engineering and design. The project technical objectives, to whatever extent established so far, have now to be defined in detail and fully developed. There can be great variation in the amount of technological planning required by a project. It can vary from almost nothing, in the case of a repeat project, to the largest project expense, when there is a high development content. Its main constituents can be listed briefly as follows:

Process definition. In systems terms the inputs and outputs for the plant are often specified in the project intent. The method of conversion from one to the other needs now to be spelled out. Typically, this is carried out in terms of a standard notation, such as flow diagrams (chemical industry), circuit diagrams (electronics) or process charts (engineering manufacture). The whole of the project content will be described in this way to obtain an overall view and to assess the interaction effects of constituent sections.

Process and engineering design. This comprises the functional and engineering design of all those project constituents for which a proprietary design is not available for technical or commercial reasons. The design need not be carried out by the firm; it can be contracted out to consultants or suppliers. But the task of verification or design approval still remains in such cases. Design in this context includes detail draughting as well as the construction of models. It can cover a wide range of technological skills. The design activity itself can be viewed as a hierarchy of complexity ranging from the total technological assembly of major units down to the last small component.

Specification development. Within our context of production plant a technical specification is a statement about the expected character of an item of equipment, including its mode of construction where this is relevant. In terms of performance it will be concerned with such aspects as size, output rates, operational speeds, accuracy, reliability, etc. A particular environment may be specified in which such a performance is to be expected. The design requirements may dwell on basic matters of construction and such features which are important for operation, safety and maintenance. Separate specifications may be needed for installation and site construction work, acceptance testing, etc. Technical specifications usually form part of the contract conditions for procurement purposes.

Equipment selection. This activity is a natural follow-on from the specification task. It can also be a concurrent activity when the technical specification is required to structure the selection process. Equipment selection is seen here primarily as a technical rather than as a commercial choice; the latter is part of the procurement task. The specification sets the profile of technical requirements; equipment selection is the shortlisting of proprietary plant which can match the chosen profile. In such a profile construction one can distinguish between primary and secondary attributes. Primary attributes are those which reflect the very purpose of the plant and as such are not regarded as 'negotiable'. The secondary attributes are concerned with desirable but not essential features, and their selection is more affected by price considerations.

In essence then, equipment selection sets the boundaries within which the procurement decision has to be made. It is of course possible with specialist applications that the boundaries leave room for only one proposition. If no proposition is left, then there is no suitable proprietary equipment and the firm may be forced to develop its own plant. With effective project preparation such a possibility should have been anticipated.

Procurement

Procurement consists of the acquisition of all plant, materials and external services required for a project. It involves the purchase of proprietary equipment, the negotiation of construction projects, indeed, anything which commits the firm in contract, be it from a small fitting to a multi-million-pound agreement. It is not confined to the buying act but includes all contractual relationships until the close of a transaction. Procurement can be responsible for over 90% of the project cash outflow. It is a key activity in the implementation stage which needs to be effectively integrated within the overall project system. Where the scale of operation warrants it, this form of procurement is organisationally separated from the purchase of materials for ongoing production operations. Within the project time scale, procurement follows the technological planning activity which, in the first instance, defines the type of equipment to be bought.

Construction

It is common project experience that as the planning work declines the centre of attention and activity shifts to the physical project execution — construction. This is no coincidence, but the logic of the project structure; construction only becomes a meaningful activity when its course has been charted, when all the relevant planning has been completed. Construction covers all building and related activities from trial test boring on a new, 'greenfield' factory site to the final landscaping. It includes the construction of production plant *in situ,* such as a new furnace, and the installation of equipment in specified positions. It can also involve temporary works such as road diversions, site workshops and construction personnel facilities. The site may be distant from the planning office; the workforce may be that of the firm or, more likely, employed by independent contractors.

The physical input of the construction activity tends to overshadow the other project implementation stages. Yet its success is largely a function of its predecessors. This does not deny the other important ingredient that has now to be furnished by the project group — effective site management. Where major construction schemes may employ hundreds, even thousands, where labour forces have to be built up, changed in mix and run down at rates which are unthinkable in most fields of production — in such cases there is a premium on the skills of work planning, coordination and control, skills which are the hallmark of good site management.

Plant integration

This is to some extent a continuation of the construction stage, and its segregation may seem somewhat artificial. Yet this work has a different emphasis. Consider walking past a public building under construction. The physical erection of the shell seems to be a comparatively quick process. This is then followed by an apparently long period when the building is there but still incomplete. This is the time when the empty shell is transformed for meaningful occupation; when the electricians, telephone people and plumbers are active. Similarly with production plant. The 'hardware' is there but it is now to be integrated into an overall production unit. The transcription can involve the feed and offtake of materials from machines, conveyors, chutes, pipes, power and control circuits, instrumentation, warning devices, etc. It is such items which change a collection of machines or process points into a complete production system. The ultimate in this is the fully-automated production unit. In a very rough sense we can say then that the construction stage is concerned with the 'brawn' of production, whereas this stage is associated with the 'brains' of the process.

Plant handover

We come now to the last phase of the project implementation stage, as defined. The capital expenditure has been incurred; a new production unit is physically ready to go into service. The handover, i.e. the change of responsibility, is from the project group to operating management. In most cases where there is this division of labour, members of the operating staff nevertheless take the opportunity to acquaint themselves with the new plant during the later stages of construction and plant integration. The nearer the plant gets to the operational state the more relevant become operational aspects and the participation of the operating groups.

In formal terms the handover takes place at an instant of time, but in practice the process can be extended. With large projects the handover can be by instalments, operating personnel move in as construction labour works itself out. The handover process can include the witnessing of tests, the calibration and setting of instruments and control devices, the physical check-out of equipment. Apart from buildings, plant, spares and accessories, the handover also covers documents which may be furnished with the equipment such as key drawings and maintenance manuals.

Project control

We have already mentioned that project implementation is an objective to be achieved within the constraints of technical and operational specifications, a project budget and timetable. The aim of project control is to ensure that these set boundaries are not overstepped. If, because of some unforeseen event, these limits have to be breached then it will be the function of the control system to warn and to inform so that steps may be taken to minimise such deviations.

The principle of control is a basic principle of management, and project control is similar to the control of any other business activity. It will differ in detail from other operational control systems for two reasons. Firstly, unless the scale of operation and the level of investment is very large, the capital project activity may be intermittent. Secondly, as we have already noted at the project preparation stage, functional responsibilities for capital projects are less clearly defined than, say, for manufacturing activities. A well-designed control system generally encompasses the following project aspects:

1. Expenditures and commitments to date, giving both totals and breakdowns to specified project accounting codes. These are compared, as far as possible, with the budget forecasts for the level of progress reached.
2. Expenditure forecasts to project completion, giving details and reasons for any overruns.
3. Progress in relation to programme.
4. Completion date forecast.
5. Project developments which might affect the technical and operational prospects of the completed plant.
6. Manpower/manhour analysis of all staff employed on the project.

The design of project reporting procedures reflects the emphasis a firm may give to these various control parameters. This also governs the manner and frequency of reporting. The first level is that of the project manager who is responsible for the detailed disposition of the project resources. The second is the top management level which monitors the overall project performance.

With the four companies the financial project control system was the most explicit. Companies C and D incorporated their control requirements in their capital expenditure manuals. Typically, project financial reports were required on a four-weekly or monthly basis. Aggregate reports on overall capital budgets and expenditures were similarly asked for from the various factories or cost centres. Other facets of reporting such as on programme progress seemed less developed. Many of the small to medium capital projects consisted of plant purchases where the company was hostage to delivery promises from suppliers. With extended deliveries the monthly progress report had little to tell. Major projects of a composite nature or with a substantial design/development content often had a specific progress reporting system linked with the monthly financial statements.

A particular facet of the overall control system was the administrative procedure relating to individual project commitments. For instance, with approved projects, company C insisted that all factory purchase requisitions were checked by head office accountants against the project proposal plant list before orders could be placed. Direct labour commitments were similarly verified by factory accountants. Company D required its factory chief accountants to make sure that prescribed practices relating to engineering contracts were followed by the appropriate staff. These concerned the placing of orders, acceptance of invoices, the precise responsibilities for installation, erection and the commissioning of plant. For contracts over £10000 instructions referred to the terms of payment, price variation formulae as well as the terms for sub-contractors. Particular attention had also to be given to the procedure and authority for ordering and accepting contract modifications and additions, the provision of site facilities and rules covering hygiene, catering, union conditions, etc. These examples suggest that administrative procedures can operate as important project control devices. They also limit the discretion available to the project manager.

Indicators of implementation performance

A review of the effectiveness of project implementation depends on supporting data. Such information is however hard to get. For a proper empirical study a set of implementation attributes would need to be established and a number of projects related to these. The great problem is to obtain the type of systematic information which provides the basis for inter-company generalisations. Samples cannot be chosen at random, the availability of data is the qualification for inclusion. The project sizes vary greatly; the politics of decision making cannot always be assumed away; behavioural aspects provide a set of variables which are difficult to isolate. We have all the complications of a multi-factor, dynamic situation. Nevertheless, despite all this some meaning can be attached to two specific indicators: time and money.

Capital costs

What follows is based on a more detailed scrutiny of the project accounts for twenty-eight new plant projects in four different companies. Projects ranged in value from just under £20000 to over £3 million (1970 prices). The ratio of actual project cost/initial project authorisation was taken as the basic financial indicator. Values greater than 1 therefore indicate an overrun. The investigation was carried out at a time when the average annual rate of inflation in terms of the index of wholesale prices for mechanical engineering products was somewhat over 2%.

The minimum observed ratio value was 0.672 and it was found here and in other cases where ratio values were appreciably below 1 that projects had been curtailed. It seems that with an extended project schedule and discrete plant units a company could change the project scope without undue disturbance losses. In such cases project authorisations are revoked, cancelling financial provisions which had not yet become commitments.

The maximum ratio value of 2.150 concerned a project with a heavy development content. Other cases of overrun also indicated development complications. Interestingly, these are not always within the company. They may be the immediate responsibility of an equipment supplier but still involve the company in consequential costs. Overall, the observations suggest that as the technical development content increases, project cost prediction also becomes more difficult. The closer a project comes to a research and development proposition the more apposite are Mansfield's findings[4] about the divergence between estimated and actual project costs. The technical risks are greater and this shows in project cost overruns. One might argue that with fuller project preparation such costs might be reduced. Admittedly, the project accounts can gain but this does not necessarily yield much of an overall saving to the company.

Irrespective of cause, project delays increased the chances of excess project costs, quite apart from inflation effects. The spread of project ratio values within a company also sheds light on its investment activities. For instance, the nine projects from one company had value ratios from 0.950 to 1.060. The company had a tight system of project financial control. Apart from one major factory scheme, however, most of its projects were of modest value, comparatively short duration and constituted mainly proprietary equipment. With a given level of organisational effectiveness, the nearer projects come to the 'shopping basket' type, the closer should the outturn be to the original estimate.

As an indicator of implementation effectiveness, project costs are a useful guide provided allowance is made for:

1. late invoices and contingent liabilities;
2. changes in project content;
3. interrelated projects where cost transfers are sometimes made for 'in-house' reasons.

The project time scale

Earlier in this chapter we included in the project implementation stage all those constituents from the project brief to the plant handover. The time lapse from the beginning of the former to the end of the latter would then constitute the project time scale. It is this parameter of project performance which we wish to consider further, both in terms of intention and of achievement.

Problems of definition. The terms: project time scale, project period, do not present serious conceptual problems, particularly if they can be related to specified systems of the type outlined in Figure 11.1. However, a number of interpretation and measurement problems affect their use in analysis. The point may be made by some examples from the twenty-eight projects studied in detail.

One project had no time schedule. It was authorised only near the end of the physical plant construction process. Commitments were undertaken on the basis of personal understandings between senior executives of the main contracting companies and their client. Work proceeded on that basis; authorisation and formal confirming orders came only towards the close of the work tasks. The detailed project correspondence left no doubt about the commitment and the implied contract, inferable from the conduct of the parties, would have been sustained in law. Whilst, perhaps, this was the most outstanding example of 'pre-authorisation commitment', similar tendencies were also noted with some other projects. Such informal commitment, before the actual board decision, reveals interesting aspects of organisational behaviour.

A further complication arose with some plant development and construction projects. In technical terms it was difficult to draw the line between development work before authorisation and the full equipment design subsequent to it. Project time scale definition became even more difficult when subsequently some of the pre-authorisation development costs were capitalised as part of the project costs. The project starting point could thus be redefined retrospectively.

At the other end of the project period technical and operating problems at the commissioning stage were the source of further difficulties. The periods of project execution and plant commissioning could overlap, particularly with those large projects where handover to production could be on a stage-by-stage basis. Failure or troubles at commissioning might force the project team and contractors to spend further time on plant modification, in some instances after they had already left the construction/installation site. Where there were no formal 'handover' documents, it was necessary to infer from the withdrawal of construction/installation labour that the project was physically complete for operational purposes.

It should not be inferred, of course, that every project time scale has such problems. However, it is important to be on one's guard when generalising from such data.

The scheduled project period. In the evaluation of the scheduled project period it is important to remember the background of a project. Where the project is confined to plant aspects and is unhampered by other time considerations, then the project schedule becomes a timetable for technological planning, procurement and installation work. The project schedule may however by affected by non-project factors.

For instance, one project concerned major plant modifications the costs of which were capitalised. An important operational requirement was to maintain at all times adequate production capacity to meet the company's sales commitments. There had to be sufficient excess plant to production requirements to release machines for modification. Because of the nature of the product and its distribution costs such excess plant could not necessarily be aggregated on a group basis, i.e. a particular factory had to be able to release a given machine. It was this which governed the project time scale, not the actual work content.

Another extraneous influence on the project time schedule is capital rationing. In one project all the plant could have been procured and installed within a few months. However, project cash release was determined by overall cash flow considerations and this more than doubled the project period.

Apart from this type of extra-project factor one can broadly relate the scheduled project period to the following:

1. the project size,
2. its technical and development content,
3. the delivery periods of key equipment.

For the reasons already stated, such relationships can only be regarded as approximate.

Time schedule performance. As with project costs a similar ratio can be used for the time dimension. It will now be the ratio of the actual to the scheduled project period. The scheduled project periods ranged from three to thirty-six months. The longest actual period noted came to sixty months but as work on it and finance for it were intermittent, the project was somewhat of a special case. About 60% of all the projects were completed to schedule. The best time ratio of 0.667 reflected project curtailment. When overruns took place they were substantial in actual and in ratio terms. Time ratios of 2.5 and 2.4 were noted for specialist but proven proprietary equipment and this exceeded the overruns of in-company development-type plant projects. Three of the four projects with major development content exceeded their schedules.

With small samples only tentative conclusions are possible. As with costs, it seems, however, that an increase in project development content makes schedule prediction more difficult. Also, delays with suppliers and contractors, irrespective of technical task content, can at times be seriously underestimated.

Check list: Project implementation

1. Who is responsible for the implementation of the project?
2. To whom does he report?
3. What personal qualities, skills and experience would you seek in a project manager, project engineer? How do you dissect his track record?
4. Does the project brief specify the total approved expenditure, the project engineering and management fee?
5. What is the specified project completion date?
6. Is the project brief otherwise clear as to what will be expected? Where a project submission includes alternatives — has the choice been made and stated?
7. Is the project manager's role clearly defined?
8. Are there standard project procedures for guidance on project planning, scheduling, coordination, costing and control practice?
9. Have the relationships between the project group and the 'project client' been examined, defined?
10. Have you carried out a project systems audit? If not, take a machine specification or a layout drawing. Who should get a copy, who should be consulted, who should approve it? Describe all aspects in a block diagram form. Are there gaps or inconsistencies?
11. What management techniques are used for project planning and control?
12. Do you ever audit the use of these techniques and look for a better cost/benefit ratio?
13. To what extent are major suppliers/contractors integrated with your project system? What is the communications framework?
14. How are the physical tasks of construction organised, managed and controlled?
15. Have relationships been adequately defined between site staff and the project section?

16. Has the handover of the completed project been sorted out?
17. How will the prospective operating staff be associated with the project prior to handover?
18. Are the methods of financial reporting and control appropriate for the project?
19. Do project reports give adequate warning of impending bottlenecks and delays?

References

1. Moder, J.J. & Phillips, C.R., *Project Management with CPM and PERT,* Reinhold Publishing Corporation, (New York, 1964)
2. Hajek, V.G., *Project Engineering,* McGraw-Hill, (New York, 1965)
3. Hackney, J.W., *Control and Management of Capital Projects,* John Wiley, (New York, 1965)
4. Mansfield, E., et al, *Research and Innovation in the Modern Corporation,* MacMillan, (London, 1972)

12 The project outcome evaluation

We now come to the final stages of the plant investment process. The project funds have been spent; results are now expected. Figure 12.1 shows the remaining activities: those concerned with the project outcome and its evaluation.

Plant commissioning

The new buildings are ready, the equipment is in position, all connections and circuits have been completed. Operating personnel are standing by to begin the plant commissioning task. It is the optimist, perhaps the layman, who would describe this activity as 'switching on'. Plant commissioning is often a complex business. Its first objective is to establish whether the installed plant works; whether it is capable of achieving the physical tasks that are expected from it. The second objective is to confirm whether the plant can work to design and operational specifications. That is a major step in the economic realisation of the project intent.

The commissioning task can have many components. With process plants, such as in the food or drug industries, it can mean thorough washing out and sterilisation. The equipment might have to be purged with inert gases, charged with catalysts or chemicals. Services, such as steam or compressed air, may have to be fed to the plant, all moving parts need to be lubricated, all control circuits and warning devices set. Operators and supervisors are often new to the type of plant. A vital stage of their training and familiarisation occurs when the detailed plant behaviour is not yet really known. Commissioning assistance may be given by plant suppliers as part of their contract. In other cases licensors may furnish specialists as part of a know-how agreement. Such staff is invaluable but expensive and often only available for limited periods. One of the great problems with large-scale process plants is the operational blending of the various sub-units. Each might operate without too much difficulty as a separate unit, but overall balance and stability is not easily achieved. To all this must be added the risks due to, and at times the damage caused by, the unexpected, the oversights, errors, carelessness and other relevant ingredients of human imperfection. Discrete production units, such as machine tools, are relatively simple to commission, but the problems compound with complex, automated equipment. If operating conditions are severe or the materials processed are dangerous then plant commissioning can be quite hazardous.

This tells in terms of time and money. Commissioning may take weeks, even months. Some plants never properly leave the commissioning stage because they fail to achieve the set operating specification. Despite modifications the plant remains 'de-rated'. During the commissioning stage the plant is in the nursery. Often it draws on the best operating and supervisory staff, in a crisis management too might stay and even work on the shop floor! Output may be erratic but costs will be consistently heavy. Commissioning expenses and delays often have an adverse effect on the first year of operation. A good project proposal makes provision for such a contingency, but accurate forecasts may be difficult to make.

Plant commissioning experiences furnish much of the

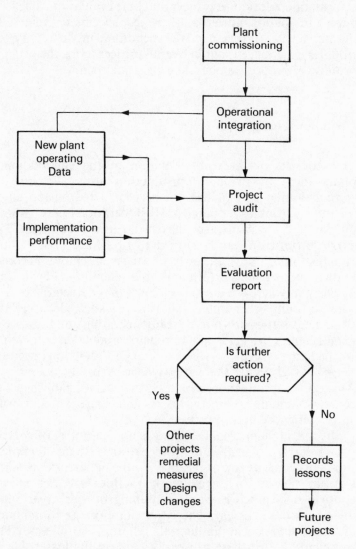

Figure 12.1 The project outcome evaluation process

information relevant to project outcome evaluation. They are one of the major indicators of project success or failure. In the latter case further capital expenditure might rectify the troubles experienced, but in overall project terms the original promise or proposition has then been qualified.

Operational integration

This consists of the transformation of the commissioned plant into an ordinary production unit. Where the commissioning process has not been afflicted by too many 'teething troubles' operational integration may follow quickly and the two stages may blend into each other. The extra attention and support provided for plant commissioning is withdrawn in stages as more becomes known about plant performance and reliability. This is particularly so where a plant shows 'burn-in' characteristics, i.e. where a number of initial failures are expected before the equipment settles down to a steady operating condition. The plant acquires the status of an ordinary production unit — it is weaned, so to speak — when special considerations need no longer be given to the various aspects of its operations. Appropriate production standards have been established and can be maintained; operating personnel are familiar with and experienced in the process.

Successful plant commissioning is no guarantee, of course, of effective operational integration. Some technical problems, such as corrosion, may not be apparent during the start-up phase. Envisaged work routines are not always confirmed in practice. Some retraining or work rearrangement may be necessary. The latter can give rise to manning disputes and other industrial relations problems. The stoppages due to these can easily outstrip the losses due to breakdowns. There can be much variation in the time scale of operational integration. Where it has led to, or has been used for, 'political embroilment', the time scale may extend to years.

When the operational integration of the new plant has been completed or all efforts have been made towards its attainment, then the last stage of the investment process has been reached. This last stage is often known as the *project audit*. It is, in essence, a total review of the project, a comparison, in all respects, of performance with promise. This chapter is mainly concerned with this last phase — the evaluation of the project outcome.

Project outcome evaluation

When we refer to the project outcome we consider all the incremental changes that can be ascribed in a total situation to the advent and completion of a particular project. This includes the operation of the plant thereby created.

Such a wide interpretation of the term 'project outcome' provides two opportunities for further exploration:

1. It includes the assessment of both quantitative and non-quantitative changes.
2. It enables as broad a comparison as possible to be made between project promise and project outcome.

Of course, the incremental changes can be numerous; for instance, in just one functional area, say manufacture, we can have changes in production rates, productivity, labour utilisation, etc. For the convenience of analysis such changes can be aggregated under the following main headings:

1. Economic changes. These are normally quantified in financial terms.
2. Technical changes. These are seen in terms of the interpretation given in Table 3.2.
3. Operational changes. These can be viewed as changes in the pattern of work organisation and the manning required for the production task.

4. Behavioural changes. We are concerned here with individual and working group relationships.

Problems of outcome evaluation

Not much has been written about the practice of project audits. We are in a difficult and somewhat sensitive area here. Systematic outcome evaluation requires a comprehensive project follow-up procedure. The main obstacles affecting the development of such a follow-up system can be summarised as follows:

1. The difficulty of isolating the purely incremental project changes from other developments in a dynamic situation.
2. Problems of result apportionment in a multi-activity setting, particularly in a conflict situation.
3. The nature of subjective judgement involved in the consideration of intangible benefit claims.
4. The implicit nature of many assumptions which underlie benefit computation.

Despite these difficulties, a certain amount of project audit can be seen in practice, particularly where the unit can be readily isolated as a profit or cost centre. Attention is also given to those project aspects which are more readily observed and measured, typically the following:

1. the project time schedule.
2. project capital cost data
3. plant performance data
4. plant manning data
5. product sales forecasts
6. product quality standards.

The nature of the plant commissioning process is often such that attention will be given to details of plant performance, particularly if these have contractual implications, such as the retention of monies. Again, if a particular project aspect shows a decisive change for the worse, then management is usually forced into a special investigation. However, apart from such cases there is little incentive for detailed investigation at the operational level if the plant satisfies the operating specifications.

The concept of investment control

The most significant attempt to put project evaluation on a systematic footing has been made by Lüder[1]. In his view investment control has two components. The first is essentially a series of project audits which evaluate the performance of a production unit over a period of years, if necessary.

His basic concept was expressed by the following relationships:

$$A = E_w - E_t = A(D, S, M)$$

where A = project outcome variance
          E_w = budgeted project outcome
          E_t = actual project outcome

Also A is a function of:

          D = degree of completeness of the project data
          S = accuracy limits of the data
          M = the degree of data manipulation

(Manipulation is not meant to be derogatory here. It refers to the transcription of data originally intended for other purposes.) These factors, in turn, are dependent on the levels of decision preparation and project control. It is difficult to measure factors such as D or M. The concept does not provide a technique but a general way of looking at projects which is helpful for comparisons.

An approach to project outcome evaluation

There are two basic project categories where the scope and worth of project evaluation seem to be in question. One is the very simple project where the task looks hardly worthwhile, particularly if the claimed benefits are obvious to all. The other is the project in a complex, fast-changing setting where the prospect of meaningful evaluation looks too daunting. Even if these categories were accepted as unrewarding, many important projects could still be evaluated to advantage.

The case for the project audit

What justifies the task of project audit? Like all instruments of review and control it must justify itself in cost/benefit terms. It is not a matter of mere curiosity nor should it be the vehicle for a witch-hunt. It is done for the information and lessons which it yields and makes available as an ingredient of future managerial decision-taking. An audit can confirm the need for corrective action. It provides guidelines for the assessment of similar, subsequent project submissions. The feedback can be used for future project preparation work, particularly where this is done away from the plant location. It has a training dimension and a tinge of discipline.

With many companies there is a large gap between the overall return on capital employed and the returns claimed for plant projects. One would have thought that a project which shows a return of only 5% or 6% is not economically justifiable. Yet when we look at capital employed which is largely an aggregate of past investment projects, including both fixed assets and working capital, then we often find such returns in practice. No doubt, there are many reasons, and scapegoats, for the difference between company and project rates of return. The ultimate yield of a project audit can be seen in the reduction of this gap.

Where a company has many projects it will be useful to specify a project value above which, in the absence of good cause, an audit shall be carried out. Below this is a sampling approach can be used. Understandably, companies are often reluctant about taking on more staff for such review duties. However, staffing aspects are less crucial where established project audit procedure reduces the task content. Where a large firm already has an internal audit section, project audit can be part of its remit. Alternatively, estimating sections and management accounting departments may already be involved in project preparation and implementation monitoring. They have much of the needed background. The project audit task can also be made part of a management development programme, where future senior staff learn more about the art of dissecting complex situations.

The timing of the project audit

The intent of the project audit is to get a fair and proper view of how a plant project turned out. It needs to be done after the operational integration when, so to speak, a 'steady state' has been reached. Before then, one could still get performance fluctuations as the plant is in the process of settling down. If it is left too long the accretions of subsequent decisions and changes need to be isolated. This becomes more difficult with time.

The substance of the project audit

The task of the project audit is to establish the project costs and returns and to compare these with the forecasts on which the project was authorised. This will then give the variance on the project return. By the time of the audit the project accounts should give a good picture of the capital expenditure incurred and the investigation could concentrate on the verification of project benefits.

Much of this will be a repetition of the original benefit computation (see Chapter 5, p.91ff.) but with actual, not expected, data. Have all the stated changes in costs actually taken place and to the amounts first specified? Have there

Table 12.1a   Sample project audit data

Item	Year 1 forecast (£)	Year 1 actual (£)	Variance (£)
Tooling	12000	7000	5000
Maintenance	9000	12000	(3000)
Consumables	6000	4000	2000
Plant services	20000	21000	(1000)
etc.	etc.	etc.	etc.
Total plant support costs	60000	57000	3000
Contribution from extra sales	100000	85000	(15000)
Cash flow	40000	28000	(12000)

Brackets denote unfavourable variances.

been unexpected changes in costs? Does the volume of output and sales differ from forecasts? Have the budgeted margins been achieved? All the ingredients of revenue and cost within the original calculation are scrutinised and deviations noted.

A project audit also has a systems aspect. Is the information system the same which furnished the original data? For instance, has the term 'departmental efficiency' the precise meaning as before? Have all the assumptions been confirmed? Consider, as an illustration, all the differences between a predicted three-shift and an actual two-shift system. Have there been cost apportionments which blur the incremental analysis? Are there any operational aspects which will require subsequent provisions, such as extra maintenance spares, or affect the expected plant life?

The result of the audit will be a report. This is more effective if it comes in a standard format. If convenient, different forms can be used for projects above or below a key value, thus reflecting different levels of scrutiny. The report summarises the main audit findings and recommendations and highlights the key points of the financial summary. Wherever possible, financial comparisons should be in con-

Table 12.1b Audit return computation

Year	Forecast cash flow (£)	Revised cash flow (£)	Variance (£)
0	(100 000)	(110 000)	(10 000)
1	40 000	28 000	(12 000)
2	30 000	27 000	(3 000)
3	30 000	27 000	(3 000)
4	25 000	22 500	(2 500)
5	25 000	22 500	(2 500)
DCF return	16.8%	5.2%	(11.6%)

stant terms, i.e. inflation effects should be segregated.

To illustrate a simple form of audit summary consider Example 1 in Chapter 5 (p.104). Assume that it is a year after the scheduled start-up date. Plant construction costs came to £110 000, project completion was delayed by a month and subsequent commissioning difficulties reduced the volume of saleable output expected for the first year of operation. Table 12.1a shows part of a revised cost and revenue computation which yields the cash flow for the year. In the light of this experience, future cash flows are now expected to be reduced by 10% over the remainder of the plant life. Table 12.1b indicates the effect this will have on project returns. It will be seen from the outcome comparison that the excess capital expenditure together with the reduced benefit cash flow has a big effect on the project return.

The audit yield

To some extent this has already been anticipated when the case for a project audit was put. It is, however, useful to list its main benefits, and these should be seen in the context of ongoing operations and not as the result of an isolated activity.

1. The audit helps to clarify the need for remedial measures. These may be operational changes or additional projects.

2. It may reinforce the case for technical/design changes with future similar plant.
3. It might make a firm more circumspect about the industrial relations and productivity bargaining aspects of a new project.
4. Future project preparation might become more rigorous with greater scrutiny of assumptions.
5. Even if everything has gone well, the project audit is a point of departure for plant performance improvement and cost reduction schemes.

The practice of outcome evaluation

Project audits are a sensitive and generally a confidential matter. This may well be why so relatively little is published about the subject. The most systematic study about its nature and prevalence has been carried out by Lüder. His investigation was into investment control, of which the audit is a part, and in this he had the cooperation of thirty-eight companies. Of these twenty-five were US firms; the remainder were German companies. Nineteen out of the twenty-five US companies and five out of the thirteen German companies had an investment project control and follow-up system. The difference between the two sets of firms is significant and is accentuated by the fact that the five German firms included subsidiaries of US companies.

Lüder found that much of the available information, being obtained initially for other purposes, was not the most appropriate for control requirements, nor was it always of the necessary quality. With most companies there was no systems evaluation focused on the furnishing of such data. Where it was available it often did not lead to corrective action. The relative shortage of suitable staff left most of the control data with the original project estimators and, whilst this had a learning function, it eroded the discipline of a separate audit.

Rockley[2] has provided some evidence of project follow-up

systems in British industry. Some firms which do have a system apply it after, say, the first year of plant operation and from this make assumptions about the overall project outcome for the remainder of the plant life. The horizon of the plant proposal is not matched by an equal time scale of retrospect. This does not mean, of course, that the firm ceases to collect data about its production plant; it will do so at the operational level for operational purposes, rather than for a time interval series of project audits. The need to gather particular information for special purposes is likely to remain. However, these no longer form part of the investment process.

Some case examples

Company A, in the engineering industry, had considered a formal project audit system but thought there were too many variables for detailed economic evaluation. Nevertheless, there was verification of specified project objectives, such as increased production rates or reduced manning levels. In that respect the original project applicants could and were held responsible for meeting such claims.

In its policy and procedure statements for capital expenditure, company C specified the follow-up investigation to be carried out by the management accounting department to ensure that anticipated savings had materialised where projects had in the first place been approved on a financial basis. Where the anticipated savings had not been achieved details of remedial action had to be submitted. Follow-up investigations had to be initiated three months after the physical project completion.

A separate follow-up procedure applied to small projects with above-average financial viability. The project procedure was confined here to proposals with a pay-off period of one year or less and where the cost savings were due to a reduction in labour or revenue expenditure costs. It did not apply to capacity expansion projects. The follow-up was scheduled to commence at the end of the pay-off period. The follow-up report was made on a special form, designed to highlight the manner of anticipated saving. For instance, it required a detailed statement of labour savings with the results alongside the estimates. Where the project did not achieve the expected savings, the capital sum was withdrawn from the special authorisation procedure and debited to the appropriate capital expenditure budget.

In company D the project review was part of the standard accounting procedure and was, in the first instance, concerned with variances in the capital costs against budget. The anticipated savings and additional revenue expenses, such as plant maintenance, had to be built into cost standards and thus provided project feedback in operating terms. Depending on their nature, expenditure reviews were the responsibility of either the divisional controllers or the group management accountant. For projects over a certain size the reviews were scheduled to take place:

1. Twelve months after the estimated commissioning date and twelve months from the actual commissioning date if more than three months later.
2. After that when any break-even point was scheduled to be met.
3. Again when full plant capacity was estimated to have been reached.

The review reports were circulated to all the original signatories and authorities to the original capital project form. The internal audit department was required in the normal course of its activities to audit some of these post-completion reviews. The review system reflected the company's evolution towards a fully-integrated planning and control system. Review experience was expected to affect targets for subsequent capital projects. Failures to meet targets would increase the required percentage returns.

It was a prime responsibility of the finance division staff to ensure that reports and action followed these reviews at the appropriate levels.

Check list: Project audit

First review

1. Has the project been completed within its authorised expenditure? If not, why not?
2. Was the project completed on time? If not, what were the reasons?
3. Is there a standard practice of plant handover?
4. Does the installed plant work?
5. Was plant commissioning within budget and time schedule?
6. Did licensors, suppliers and contractors fulfil their commissioning obligations?
7. Has all the plant been accepted?
8. Where plant has proved unsatisfactory have any monies been retained, any redress sought?
9. What were the greatest commissioning problems, surprises?
10. Does the plant work to design and operating specifications?
11. Did operating procedures have to be changed because of commissioning experience? What effects will this have on costs, efficiencies?
12. Was operator and supervisory training adequate?
13. Have any unexpected safety hazards come to light? If so, what is being done about them?
14. What industrial relations problems have been encountered and what lessons have been drawn for future projects?

The main performance audit

15. Who should carry this out? Why?
16. When should it be undertaken?
17. What documentation exists for project audits?
18. Has the plant kept its performance promise in terms of efficiency, production rates, cost standards?

19. Have the expected manning levels been achieved? If not, what are the major problems?
20. Have product sales predictions materialised?
21. Have the project cash flows met forecasts?
22. What are the reasons for cash flow variances?
23. Have product quality standards been achieved?
24. What contingent problems or losses have been discovered?
25. What use is made of audit reports to help future projects?

References

1. Lüder, K., *Investitionskontrolle,* Betriebswirtschaftlicher Verlag Dr. Th. Gabler, (Wiesbaden, 1969)
2. Rockley, L.E., *Capital Investment Decisions,* Business Books Ltd, (London, 1968)

Appendix A - case studies

Case study 1 — Integrated Components Ltd

The introduction of numerically controlled machine tools

Integrated Components Ltd is a major component supplier to the car and engineering industries. It employs about 5000 people and has factories in the London area, Yorkshire and South Wales. Its main product is a vital, precision engine part and this involves the company at the product design stage in advising on the design, features and materials most likely to meet the requirements of a particular application. Effective application engineering, particularly for the original equipment manufacturer, is a basic marketing policy. The success of this policy has made the company the largest specialist supplier in Europe with annual sales of about £20 million. Over the previous five years the return on the total capital employed ranged from 9% to 14% with margins on sales fluctuating between 6% and 9%.

Difficult product application problems led to exacting technical product and production specifications. Conventional production plant was found inadequate for such requirements and this encouraged the company to develop its own, special-purpose machinery. The company had now a substantial machinery design and building division which changed from a manufacturing service to a substantial business in its own right with export machinery sales and a significant licensing income.

Some of the heavier components made in the Welsh factory had a sales pattern which required small/medium batch production with the most frequent batch sizes in the 50-150 range. Production was still carried out on a line of ageing, conventional equipment and could consist of up to thirty operations per part. The machine setting time/operation/batch could exceed total operating times. The overall production cycle could be up to eight weeks, most of this consisting of work-in-progress waiting time.

It was proposed to develop and build a new range of numerically-controlled machine tools to replace the existing equipment. (Such a machine carries out exactly the same operations as a conventional unit. However, it works automatically when actuated by a programme through its control system.) There were no illusions about the heavy development costs which would be incurred but these could be justified if the following objectives could be achieved:

(a)   to eliminate the heavy work setting up costs with current methods;
(b)   to reduce/eliminate the existing level of operator skill and discretion;
(c)   by faster and simpler operation, to increase output rates by about 50% within the given floor space;
(d)   to improve the quality of work;
(e)   to simplify manufacturing methods and tooling;
(f)   to minimise loading, unloading and machine cycle times;
(g)   to reduce the amount of re-work and scrap;
(h)   to minimise planning work at shop level.

Currently average batch setting times are about 40% of the production time per operation. Setters are earning about 20% above the average rate for production workers. Direct manufacturing costs could broadly be divided into: materials 30%, setting-up labour 30%, production labour 40%. An operator hour of saleable production is valued at £7.50, average production labour costs are £2.50 per hour. Machine capacity utilisation averages about 25%.

The capital expenditure proposal

The initial design and development project met a number of difficulties and it took about two years before technically feasible equipment could be put forward for the specified production requirements. The definitive proposals included the detailed design, building and installation of twelve machine units of which eight would handle about 95% of the current output. About a third of the existing machining capacity would remain to deal with special items. A separate production area within the factory would be provided because higher standards of housekeeping were necessary. Operators would have to be retrained and some new ones recruited.

The project financial summary is appended. The reduction in direct labour costs seems now to be less significant than the increased capacity due to faster production rates. Although there were significant fluctuations, sales had grown at about 10% per annum in real terms. However, as the sales department was unwilling to forecast for more than eighteen months ahead, a growth rate of 5% was assumed for the next seven years. The extra capacity provided by the new methods and equipment was estimated at 30%. At present, capacity is broadly in line with sales.

Project financial and economic data

Project costs

Capital cost of installed equipment	£1250000
Estimated design and development costs	200000
Increase in raw material stocks	30000
Additional work in progress	40000
Increase in debtors	60000

Operating data

Only incremental changes are given. All figures are per annum annum

Contribution from extra capacity available (at standard costs)	450000
Saving in direct labour	30000
Extra indirect labour; programming, maintenance	50000
Reduction in scrap and rectification work	40000
Additional consumables	25000
Initial running-in expenses and training costs (for the first two years of operation)	30000

Notes

1. Expected plant life   10 years
2. Depreciation   10% straight line
3. Operating values and working capital requirements are expected to follow the growth of sales until full capacity is reached.

Questions

1. You are the decision maker:
   (a) Indicate what additional information or assurances you require.
   (b) What is your decision? What are its supporting arguments?
2. The works convenor of the South Wales factory has 50% of his members in the affected production area. Rumours have made his members restless. Put yourself into his shoes and outline how you would handle the situation.

Case study 2 — The British Meat Corporation Ltd

The meat loaf can project

The British Meat Corporation is a major food business with extensive manufacturing interests in the United Kingdom and Europe. Because of the scale of its operations it has been able to make its own food cans under licence from an international can manufacturer. This firm also supplies the equipment needed for can making. The northern division is interested in packing beef from a newly developed area in North Scotland. Local conditions yield a good-quality meat but of a flavour which makes the product life uncertain after about five years. Can manufacture is the responsibility of the engineering division which operates as a separate business. It has just negotiated a five-year supply contract but does not expect further business after its expiry.

A new form of square meat can is involved which requires a special quick-release body closure. The proposed can is in the 250-gram size and all its manufacturing operations, apart from the body closure, are conventional. Although high-speed closure techniques are well known and proven equipment has been used for many years, the rigid closure specification for the new can requires the purchase of special machinery.

There is the choice of two closure processes. The first, embodied in machine A, is, in essence, a high-speed soldering line. Output rates average 2,000 cans/hour, but there is the substantial cost of the solder which consists mainly of tin. The alternative is a resistance welding unit, machine B, which has an output of 1,000 cans/hour but saves the solder.

A meeting is scheduled for next week to plan the production of the new can and to confirm equipment schedules. The board has made £250000 available for capital expenditure. Additional plant purchases have to be financed from the project cash flow. A staff engineer and the divisional management accountant have prepared the following information:

Planning data — meat loaf project

1. Machine A: net installed cost: £16000. Plant life: three years.
   Machine B: net installed cost: £10000. Plant life: two years.
2. For smooth operation equipment will have to be installed at the beginning of the production year.
3. The scrap value of the worn-out equipment is balanced by the cost of its removal.
4. Confirmed output rates from supplier:
       Machine A: 2000 cans/hour
       Machine B: 1000 cans/hour
5. We have made the following planning assumptions:
   (a) The production year will be fifty weeks at forty hours each.
   (b) There will be no shift or overtime working.
   (c) The quoted machine output rates cover all efficiency factors.
6. The cans will be assembled in boxes of 1000 cans each.
7. The manufacturing costs with process A will be £18 per

box (see extra for solder); for process B they will be £24 per box.

8. The solder material costs have to be added to process A. One ton of tin provides solder for 1000 boxes. The material cost per box is about £1 per £1000 of the price of tin. Tin prices fluctuate but we estimate that the current price of £6000 per ton will increase at the rate of 8% per annum over the next five years.

9. Our pattern of manufacturing costs is such that unused capacity incurs annual losses equivalent to machine depreciation on a pro-rata basis.

The agreed price for the supply of cans is £30 per box. The contract calls for the following supply schedule:

Year	Boxes per week
1	1000
2	1100
3	1200
4	1300
5	700

The board expects a return of 15% after tax on its investments. Corporation tax is 52% and investment allowances are 100%. It is your task to make equipment proposals at the meeting. As your figures might be challenged you have been advised to complete and table the attached project evaluation summary form (Enclosure A).

Questions

1. What will be your equipment strategy?
2. How profitable will the project be on that basis?
3. What will be the equipment life-cycle costs over the period of five years?

Enclosure 'A'

The British Meat Corporation

Project evaluation summary-sheet 1

Year	0	1	2	3	4	5	6
Machine A No.							
Machine B No.							
Capital expenditure (£)							
Allowances cash flow							
Total production capacity (boxes per week)							
Sales volume (boxes per week)							
Annual sales (£)							
Standard factory cost of sales (£)							
Raw material costs (process A) (£)							
Other expenses or gains (please list)							
Net annual revenue (£)							
Corporation tax (£)							
Overall cash flow (£)							
Discount factors at 15%	1.00	.87	.76	.66	.57	.50	.43
Discounted cash flow							
Cumulative project NPV (£)							
Life-cycle cost (£)							

Appendix B - discount factors

The present value of £1 after 'n' years when discounted at a rate of interest 'r'%

$n \downarrow$	$r \rightarrow 1\%$	2%	3%	4%	5%	6%	7%	8%	9%	10%	11%	12%
1	.990	.980	.971	.962	.952	.943	.935	.926	.917	.909	.901	.893
2	.980	.961	.943	.925	.907	.890	.873	.857	.842	.826	.812	.797
3	.970	.942	.915	.889	.864	.840	.816	.794	.772	.751	.731	.712
4	.961	.924	.889	.855	.823	.792	.763	.735	.708	.683	.659	.636
5	.952	.906	.863	.820	.784	.747	.713	.680	.650	.621	.593	.567
6	.942	.888	.834	.790	.746	.705	.666	.630	.597	.565	.535	.507
7	.933	.870	.813	.760	.711	.665	.623	.584	.547	.513	.482	.452
8	.924	.854	.789	.731	.677	.627	.582	.540	.502	.466	.434	.404
9	.914	.837	.766	.703	.645	.592	.544	.500	.460	.424	.391	.361
10	.905	.820	.744	.676	.614	.558	.508	.463	.422	.386	.352	.322
11	.896	.804	.722	.650	.585	.527	.475	.420	.388	.351	.317	.288
12	.887	.789	.701	.625	.557	.497	.440	.397	.356	.319	.286	.257

The present value of £1 after 'n' years when discounted at a rate of interest 'r' %

$n \downarrow$ / $r \to$	13%	14%	15%	16%	17%	18%	19%	20%	25%	30%	40%	50%
1	.885	.877	.870	.862	.855	.848	.840	.833	.800	.770	.714	.667
2	.783	.770	.756	.743	.731	.718	.706	.694	.640	.592	.510	.444
3	.693	.675	.658	.641	.642	.609	.593	.579	.512	.455	.364	.296
4	.613	.592	.572	.552	.534	.516	.499	.482	.410	.350	.260	.198
5	.543	.519	.497	.476	.456	.437	.419	.402	.328	.269	.186	.132
6	.480	.456	.432	.410	.390	.370	.352	.335	.262	.207	.133	.088
7	.425	.400	.376	.354	.333	.314	.296	.279	.210	.159	.095	.059
8	.376	.350	.327	.305	.285	.266	.249	.233	.168	.123	.068	.039
9	.333	.308	.284	.263	.243	.226	.209	.194	.134	.094	.048	.026
10	.295	.270	.247	.227	.208	.191	.176	.162	.107	.073	.035	.017
11	.261	.237	.215	.195	.178	.162	.148	.135	.086	.056	.025	.012
12	.231	.208	.187	.169	.152	.137	.124	.112	.069	.043	.018	.008

Index